I0762701

Homage to Aert van der Neer
向阿爾特 · 范 · 德 · 尼爾致敬

Alberto Reguera
艾拔圖 · 雷古拉

香 港 大 學 美 術 博 物 館
University Museum and Art Gallery
The University of Hong Kong

Published for the exhibition *Alberto Reguera: Homage to Aert van der Neer*
at the University Museum and Art Gallery, The University of Hong Kong,
18 January-30 April 2023.

本書是香港大學美術博物館為配合「艾拔圖・雷古拉：向阿爾特・范・德・尼爾致敬」專題展覽而編製，該展覽展期為2023年1月18日至4月30日。

Curator 策展人
Florian Knothe 羅諾德

Designer 設計師
Stephy Tsui 徐曉雯

Translation and Editing 翻譯及編輯
Elena Cheung 張寶儀
Jessica Yeung 楊慧儀
Christopher Mattison 馬德松
Hua Shuo 華碩

Edition 版次

ISBN 國際標準書號
978-988-74707-7-9

UNIVERSITY MUSEUM AND ART GALLERY,
THE UNIVERSITY OF HONG KONG
90 Bonham Road, Hong Kong
香港大學美術博物館
香港般咸道九十號

Organised by 主辦

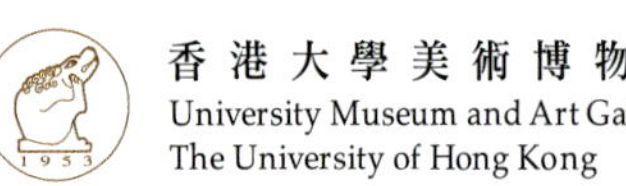

Supported by 支持

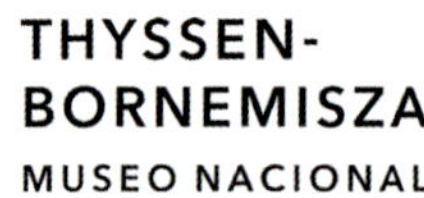

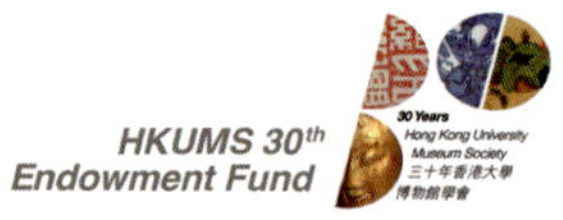

CONTENTS 目錄

7 FOREWORD 前言
Florian Knothe 羅諾德

11 HOMAGE TO AERT VAN DER NEER 向阿爾特 · 范 · 德 · 尼爾致敬
Alberto Reguera 艾拔圖 · 雷古拉

19 A CONVERSATION WITH ALBERTO REGUERA 與藝術家艾拔圖 · 雷古拉對話
Guillermo Solana 基里爾莫 · 蘇蘭納

32 CATALOGUE 作品圖版

65 BIOGRAPHY 簡歷

69 LIST OF PAINTINGS 畫目

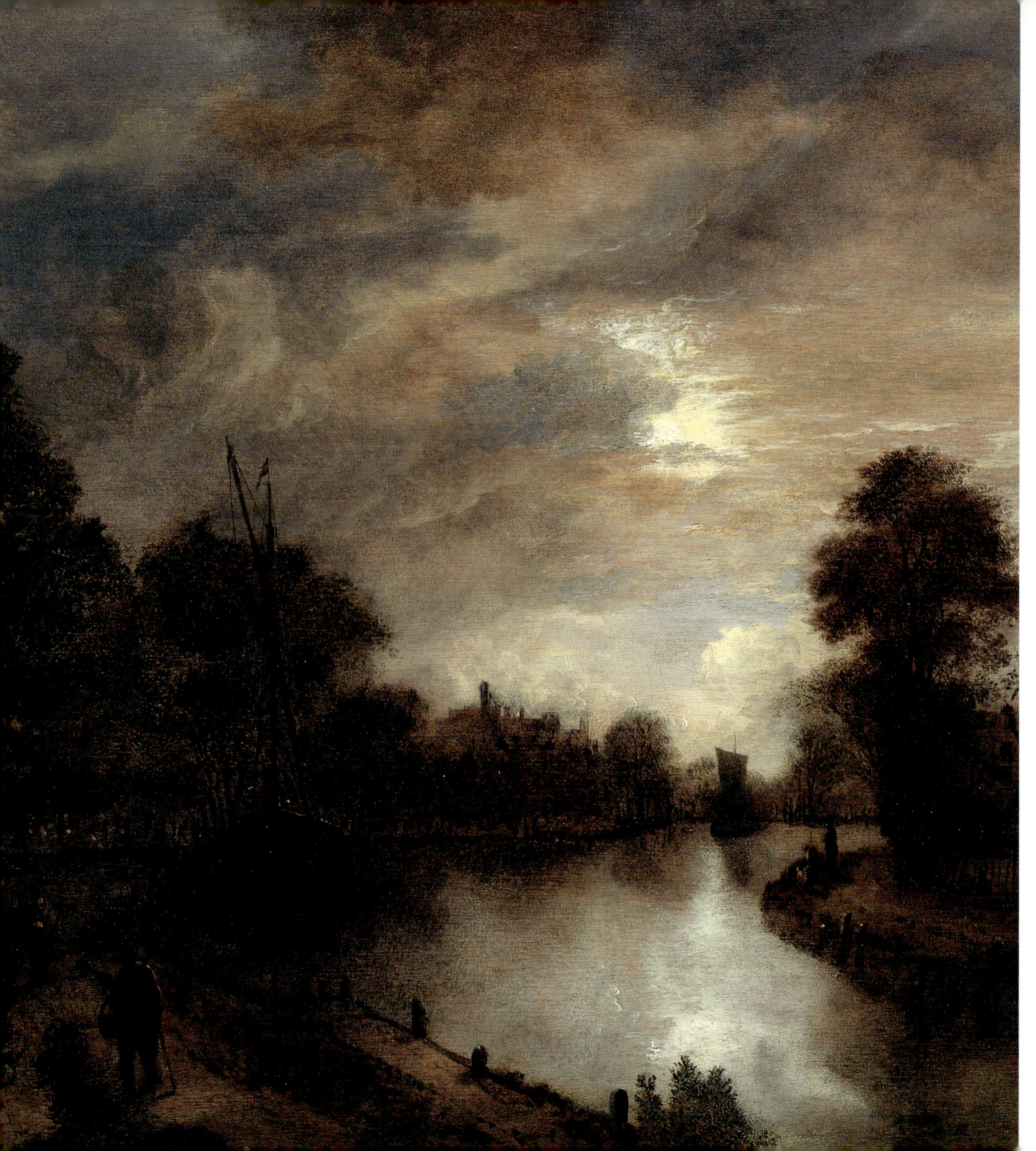

Foreword

Dazzled by the twilight of 17th-century painter Aert van der Neer's (1603–77) *Moonlit Landscape with a Road beside a Canal* (1645–50), contemporary Spanish artist Alberto Reguera created a new series of paintings as an homage to the celebrated artist of the Dutch Golden Age. Each of Reguera's paintings display an in-depth study of the representation of light and sky in the European tradition of painting, while engaging in a dialogue with Van der Neer's *Moonlit Landscape*.

Aert van der Neer's works exemplify the naturalistic renderings that are now recognised as one of the hallmarks of Dutch painting. Dating to the most productive period of the artist's life (1640–60), aspects of this scene are typical for Van der Neer and his contemporaries, while the artist's specific manipulation of twilight seeping through the clouds sets the work apart from other painters of his era.

The sensitive depiction of light in the night sky most inspired Alberto Reguera, in part because of the similarities to his own work. These new works examine and connect directly to Van der Neer's masterpiece, and the important painterly achievements of the Dutch painter's generation. While the Golden Age landscapes have been widely discussed and imitated over the past three centuries, it is Reguera's particularly intense form of study and thoughtful application of style that has culminated in these highly personal and accomplished works. Reguera's own depictions of the sky—both day and night—inevitably differ from the Dutch master, as Reguera incorporates his own sensibilities and experiences from throughout his internationally renowned career.

前言

西班牙當代藝術家艾拔圖・雷古拉為名作《皓月河旁徑》(1645–50年)所描繪之暮色而著迷。此作品由十七世紀荷蘭黃金時代畫家阿爾特・范・德・尼爾(1603–77年)所繪。為了向這位名家致敬,雷古拉繪畫全新畫作,每幅皆展現出這位藝術家對歐洲繪畫傳統所描繪之光線以及對天空的深度研究,從而跨越時空與范・德・尼爾的《皓月河旁徑》對話。

阿爾特・范・德・尼爾畫作所呈現的自然主義畫風,如今被視爲荷蘭繪畫的重要標誌之一。在范・德・尼爾創作的全盛時期(1640–60年),這些自然景致是他及其同時代畫家常用的典型題材。而他的作品之所以與衆不同,是由於他對黃昏月色穿透雲層的細膩處理手法。

《皓月河旁徑》格外喚起雷古拉的創作靈感,是因爲此作裏夜空中光線的細膩捕捉與自己的作品相彷。雷古拉的新作源於對此名畫的研究,以及呼應與范・德・尼爾同時期畫家在繪畫上所取得的矚目成果。儘管在過去三個世紀,黃金時代的風景畫受到廣泛的討論及模仿,雷古拉對藝術的琢磨及深思熟慮的筆觸造詣,成就出這些甚具個人風格的精品。有異於其他荷蘭繪畫大師,他所演繹的晝夜天色,均融合個人的感悟,以及他在國際藝壇成就提煉出的經驗。

The exhibition and accompanying publication is the second collaboration between the University Museum and Art Gallery and Alberto Reguera. While the first exhibition *Blue Expansive Landscape* (2015) was notable for the display of the painter's two- and three-dimensional works, and his innovative ways of painting beyond the canvas, *Homage to Aert van der Neer* is a similarly complex endeavour that has been achieved through a successful partnership with UMAG, the Museo Nacional Thyssen-Bornemisza and the artist. We thank the director and colleagues from the Museo Nacional and Alberto Reguera for this international cooperation, and express our gratitude to the University of Hong Kong Museum Society for its financial support.

Dr Florian Knothe
Director, University Museum and Art Gallery
The University of Hong Kong

這次展覽及圖錄是香港大學美術博物館與雷古拉的第二次合作，首次展覽名為「悠藍青境」(2015年)，展出了平面和立體作品，呈現藝術家令畫作延伸至畫布以外的空間。「向阿爾特・范・德・尼爾致敬」展覽與上次展覽同樣豐富，由香港大學美術博物館、提森-博內米薩國家博物館及雷古拉本人三方合作促成。本館特別感謝提森-博內米薩國家博物館總監及同事，以及艾拔圖・雷古拉，成就這次國際合作，並承蒙香港大學博物館學會的慷慨贊助，謹此致上衷心謝意。

羅諾德博士
香港大學美術博物館總監

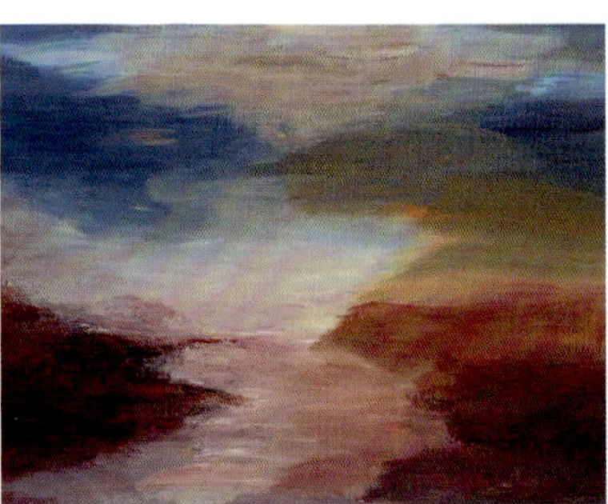

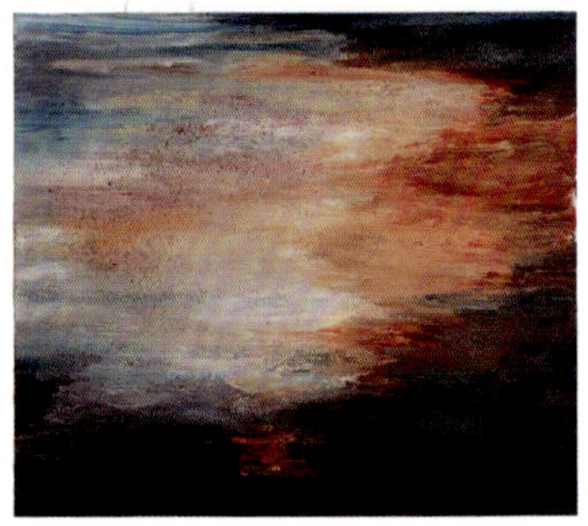

Homage to Aert van der Neer

The idea began with a painting in the permanent collection of the Museo Nacional Thyssen-Bornemisza in Madrid, Spain—*Moonlit Landscape with a Road beside a Canal* (ca. 1645–50) by the Dutch painter Aert van der Neer (Amsterdam 1603–77). Reflecting on this single painting, I made the new series of works constructed around two primary attributes: the landscape's formal support and its essential content, bearing in mind that the original had been made during the 1630s, at a time when the landscape tradition in Holland was undergoing significant transformations.

The Thyssen collection of Dutch Golden Age paintings is one of the museum's strengths, with works by Rembrandt, Frans Hals, Gerard ter Borch, Pieter Claesz and Pieter Saenredam. The museum houses three paintings by Aert van der Neer, but I have always been drawn to this moonlit landscape since the museum opened its doors in Madrid in 1992. It is hard to rationalize why I felt such a strong affinity for this particular painting; quite simply, I was amazed by the luminous power of a work so small in stature, but with such enormous charisma; I was dazzled by its depth. I am aware that, because of its diminutive size, Van der Neer's night landscape has likely been overlooked among the masterpieces by more famous painters, such as Jacob van Ruisdael and his family members. But my admiration and sense of familiarity with this painting has grown steadily with my frequent visits to the museum.

Originally created for an exhibition at the Museo Thyssen-Bornemisza, my series is indicative of both creative and professional pursuits. I prefer to develop exhibitions based on my itinerant vocation, so that each exhibition reveals a specific aspect of my

向阿爾特·范·德·尼爾致敬

這一油畫系列的創作靈感來自荷蘭繪畫大師阿爾特·范·德·尼爾（阿姆斯特丹，1603–77年）的名作《皓月河旁徑》（約1645–50年）。該作品是提森-博內米薩國家博物館的館藏。我對這一幅畫作的琢磨，造就出一系列新作，尤其是名作中對風景的構造和主題內容的表達形式。值得一提的是，《皓月河旁徑》繪於1630年代，當時荷蘭風景畫正經歷重大轉變。

荷蘭黃金時代繪畫是提森-博內米薩國家博物館最重要的收藏之一，當中作品來自倫勃朗、佛蘭斯·哈爾斯、謝拉德·特·鮑爾赫、比得·克拉斯、比得·山里德南等大師佳作。雖然館內藏有三幅范·德·尼爾的作品，但自1992年於馬德里開館以來，我每次參觀都被《皓月河旁徑》深深吸引。這很難從理性的角度解釋我何以為之心醉神迷。總而言之，如此小巧的作品能夠如此光芒四射，又具有如此驚人魅力，實在令我深感佩服之餘，構圖深度亦使我悠然神往。我注意到該畫體積細小，比起其他更著名的大師之作——如雅各布·范·勒伊斯達爾與其家族成員的作品，更易被受忽視。但隨著我經常參觀提森-博內米薩國家博物館，我對這幅畫愈發欽佩和熟悉。

oeuvre, which emerges depending on the individual project. For this reason, I continue to simultaneously develop artworks that contain expansive forms of painting and pictorial installations: large abstract three-dimensional landscapes, photography, video exhibitions and pictorial performances. In each of these modes, the space (inside or outside the painting) is instrumental in establishing the layers of visual depth.

The exhibition's core presents pictorial variations of Van der Neer's sky, conceived as a space of visual depth and contrasts. Sometimes calm and balanced, neither pure shadow nor light; sometimes intentionally heightened, as in *Una noche luminosa* (Illuminated Night), with the aim of capturing twilight fragments as a prelude to a dazzling scene. This is aided by the use of diverse pigments that also emanate light.

A key structural point is that none of the new paintings' frames are completely flat, which accentuates one of the defining characteristics of my work—layers of volume added to abstract landscapes—which in this case parallels the thickness of Van der Neer's frame. The fact that his painting is a landscape mounted to an object of considerable thickness led me to create similarly substantial frame edges. Furthermore, all of the works have been developed on rectangular formats based roughly on the original size of the Dutch painter's work.

The content and essence of Van der Neer's *Moonlit Landscape* inspired me to create a series rather than a single response; I wanted to offer each of my paintings its own personality, while establishing a visual sequence in which viewers were allowed to follow the exhibition's main thread back to Van der Neer's original work. In this Dutch master I saw a precedent that evokes the French 'Clair de lune' in artists such as Vernet. In relation to this particular French connection, Van der Neer's moonlight

我這套全新畫作系列本為提森-博內米薩國家博物館的一個展覽而作，希望能夠體現我對創意和專業的追求。我較喜歡以職業巡迴的方式創作，讓每個展覽都能夠通過個別項目而呈現作品獨特的創作理念。因此，我同時持續創作延展畫和裝置畫，包括大型抽象立體風景畫、攝影作品、錄像展覽及圖像表演藝術。不論是哪種形式，畫內畫外的空間都能建立視覺深度層次。

這次展覽的重點，是把范．德．尼爾畫筆下的天空詮釋為富有視覺深度和對比的空間，並呈現這空間的視覺變化。畫作效果時而安寧和平衡，既非純光，亦非純影，時而調高亮度。例如在畫作《亮夜》中，我運用不同顯亮的顏料，捕捉黃昏疏落的光線，以此描繪扣人心弦的夜色前奏。

這一系列新作品的結構特色，就是畫框無一是單純平面。這突出了我的作品中重要的元素——以層層的顏料複疊在抽象風景畫之上，這正好與范．德．尼爾所採用的畫框厚度互相輝映。其風景畫裝裱於厚重畫框內的作法，啟發我採用類似的厚畫框來裝飾新作。此外，所有作品之所以沿用矩形格式，是因為我大致參考了《皓月河旁徑》原作之尺寸。

受范．德．尼爾《皓月河旁徑》的主題內容和精髓啟發，我創作時以系列成組而非單一方式來回應名家之作，希望賦予每一幅作品獨特的個性，並建立視覺序列，鼓勵觀

reflecting on a canal is reminiscent of Monet's aquatic reflections. It also brought to mind the glittering water of Amsterdam's canals, which I walked in the 1990s, and which inspired me to create a series of paintings named after these canals.

Heading further along the Impressionist path, it might seem a bit presumptuous to suggest that this Dutch master anticipated, or already sensed, the 'visual agnosia' of the French painters—witnessing a landscape and then representing it in a non-objective way. The idea of bringing together, in a single painting, references to diverse landscapes is in accord with my own methods; whenever I attempt to reflect fragments on canvas, nature's more abstract facets inevitably appear.

The idea of clouds and emptiness—not as nonexistence but as a state of abundance—is another foundational layer that links back to the chromatic results of Van der Neer's clouds. Present in all of my paintings are opaque stratocumulus forms that transition towards translucence, sometimes offering a glimpse of the moon's contour. I have attempted to interpret the same sensation of celestial dynamism achieved in Van der Neer's work by creating clouds that show a diversity of celestial scenarios. One of these paintings, *Difracciones lunares* (Lunar Diffractions), takes as its reference the atmospheric phenomenon after which the piece is titled.

In some of the works, I first 'approached' the clouds I saw in the Dutch artist's painting, chose the fragments that most interested me and then enlarged them so that they could be abstracted. This is seen in the painting *Ampliadas visiones celestes* (Amplified Visions of the Sky). Within these imagined and abstracted clouds, two families of colour take precedence—pigments that give prominence to the collection's nocturnal character, ranging from Prussian blue to Payne's grey, along with turquoise,

眾根據展覽的主線，重返原作《皓月河旁徑》。我在這位荷蘭大師身上，看到他的傑作如何啟迪克勞德．韋爾內等法國「月光派」畫家。關於這個法國的聯繫，范．德．尼爾畫中月光在河上的映照，讓人聯想起莫奈的水映光線。我於上世紀九十年代在阿姆斯特丹運河旁散步的回憶，啟發我創作這些以運河為名的畫作系列。

沿著印象派的發展脈絡，不難想像這位荷蘭大師或已預料到日後法國畫家採用的「視覺失認」——即把眼前風景以非客觀的方法呈現。我嘗試用自己的畫法，把截然不同的風景入畫，每當我反復斟酌畫布上零碎的景象時，一幕幕大自然抽象片段便會湧現出來。

在我這件作品中，「雲」和「空」並非指「虛無」，而是指「豐盛」——意思是另一基礎層來銜接范．德．尼爾畫中的雲彩。這個系列的畫作都繪有層積雲，該雲層由不透明過渡至半透明，令月亮的輪廓若隱若現。為了營造范．德．尼爾作品中豐富的天象變化所衍生的感知，我嘗試透過描繪變幻莫測的天光雲影，來呈現不斷變化著的天空之景。畫作《月光衍射》便以捕捉天象氣氛為主題。

在一些作品中，我嘗試先「靠近」這位荷蘭名家畫筆下的雲彩，挑選我最感興趣的片段來描繪，然後再放大至抽象形態。《放大天像》就是這樣畫成的。這些虛構兼抽象的雲彩主要有兩組顏色，所選顏料賦予整個系

cerulean, Capri and Yale blues mixed with various shades of grey. Secondly, I employed natural earth tones and burgundy browns. All of these are tinted on the canvas with quinacridone violet and alizarin crimson. Illuminated by titanium white pigments, the colours are transformed into tawny ochres and toasted siennas. The third group of pigments are the metallics—copper and various iridescent hues which I use to make silver and gold.

These works are also meant to allude to the phenomenon of synaesthesia, as they bring me back to the chromatic fantasies of the Dutch baroque musician Jan Pieterszoon Sweelinck. In fact, some of the smaller works in the series are titled after his musical composition. Other pieces were painted while listening to the musical work of Unico Wilhelm van Wassenaer in an attempt to conjoin music and landscape. Related to this, a few years ago the contemporary Dutch musician Bart Spaan wrote several musical compositions inspired by my paintings. They were performed on two separate occasions—once by Spaan and once by the Dutch pianist Ralph van Raat. This performance took place at the Stedelijk Museum in Amsterdam, where my works were being exhibited.

Taking back up this thread of inspiration—in terms of content and essence—the series is meant to reference a specific pictorial moment that took place in the 1630s in Holland, when the foundation of landscape compositions had begun to shift, and artists working within this particular mode gave greater prominence to the celestial elements in their pictorial compositions; as a result, the horizon appears almost at the base of some paintings, presenting highly atmospheric and epic scenes whose nuances and variations continue to inspire.

列一種夜幕低垂的意境。當中的一組色彩範圍涵蓋普魯士藍至佩恩灰，與綠松色、蔚藍色、天藍色、耶魯藍並用，也配上深淺不一的灰色。另一組是自然泥土色調及接近酒紅色的棕色調。我把這些顏色與酞菁紫紅和茜草深紅一起塗於畫布上，更利用鈦白顏料的反光效果，使顏色轉化成赭褐色和赭紅色。第三組顏料具金屬色調，包括紅銅色和其他閃光色調，用來調和出金、銀兩色。

荷蘭巴洛克時期的音樂家揚・彼德松・思維林克喚起我經狂想曲之啟發而獲得的色彩聯想，因此我是存心把這系列作品引發觀者聯覺體驗。事實上，新作系列裏有部分體積較小的作品以思維林克創作的樂曲命名，另有一些作品，則是我一邊聽著荷蘭作曲家尤奈高・威林・瓦瑟納爾的作品而一邊創作，試圖結合音樂與風景畫。幾年前，荷蘭當代音樂家伯德・史班受我的作品啟發而作了幾首樂曲，並在兩個場合演出：一次由史班本人演奏，另一次則由荷蘭鋼琴家洛夫・范・拉得演奏。當時我的畫作也正在他們的演出場地阿姆斯特丹市立博物館內展出。

這次展覽的全新畫作系列延續上述展覽項目的內容和精神，紀念1630年代荷蘭繪畫史的關鍵時期。當時風景畫的基礎構圖形式正在轉變。風景畫家在構圖上強調天象元素。因此，他們把地平線設定在臨近構圖底部的位置。這些富有情調與詩意的佳作，細節精美，畫面變化萬千，至今仍是人們的靈感泉源。

In the 1630s, a number of Dutch painters created compositions with gradations of three coloured bands as a way to create depth. In the lower section of the painting were warmer and earthy colours. In the middle, greens, on which a landscape was sometimes set. And then in the upper band one could find colder blues that gave rise to feelings of emotional remoteness and physical distance. This formula faded over the following decades. Aspiring to widen the landscape's vision, these Dutch artists shifted the horizon to the lower third of the painting. The colder colours were used to highlight atmospheric qualities and the softer hues were employed within chiaroscuro to depict a harmony with the clouds.

I choose to highlight the essential importance of light in these works. The luminosity developed in the skies stretches throughout the paintings, so that both the land and water, which are placed quite low on the horizon, act as a chromatic mirror, receiving light from the sky and imparting a visual unity to the entire landscape.

Aert van der Neer was one of the influential Dutch landscape painters who employed this technique of capturing light. Often viewed from an elevated vantage point, these celestial scenes vanish into the distance and convey layers of depth. The rectangular format also allowed for more space to be given over to the sky, which added to the sense of monumentality. Obviously, there were parallel developments in Dutch painting from this time—genres including portraits and still lifes—but I have always felt more of an affinity for Van der Neer and the painters who gave priority to the epic atmospheres in their works.

1630年代，一些荷蘭畫家透過三種色域的漸變效果來營造景深：畫面底部使用暖色和褐土色調；風景主題通常置在畫面中央，多施以綠色；頂部色域則以冷色調的藍色為主，製造感覺上與實物的距離。往後幾十年，荷蘭畫家陸續摒棄上述畫法，繼而將地平線移至畫面底部三分一的位置，延伸風景的空間感，同時使用冷色來強調空氣所營造的氛圍，並在明暗對照的細部中夾雜較為柔和的色調，製造和諧的彩雲視效。

在這些作品中，我強調光線的重要性。將天上的光度伸延至整個畫面，並把地平線底部的地面和水面化成彩色明鏡，反射從天而降的光束，賦予整幅風景畫視覺上的統一。

作為最有影響力的荷蘭風景畫大師之一，范．德．尼爾採用上述的畫法捕捉光線，時常把視點設得較高，從而顯得天象高遠，畫面從視線中消失，呈現豐富的層次。況且，天空在矩形的畫框內可佔更大空間，亦往往能夠給予畫作一種雄偉的氣魄。當時荷蘭繪畫固然在各方面均有發展，無論是肖像畫或靜物畫亦然，但我仍鍾情於注重描繪史詩般氣氛的范．德．尼爾和其他畫家們的佳作。

現在讓我們再次將注意力集中於《皓月河旁徑》，須想像置身當晚當地，才能了解這位荷蘭名家如何觀察和記錄當時的夜色。畫家彷彿在高空翱翔，穿梭於畫中風景，凝視著伸延至無盡之處的地平線。這正是我嘗試在《燦爛地平線》呈現的效果。

Refocusing on the Dutch painter's *Moonlit Landscape*, it is necessary to journey through the actual air of the night scene; to be able to imagine the work of the Dutch artist as a snapshot captured by his gaze, as if he had just flown over the painted landscape from a great height, envisioning unlimited horizons. This is precisely what I have tried to reflect in *Horizontes luminosos* (Luminous Horizons).

And then while musing on Aert van der Neer, other painters from this period come to mind, such as Jacob van Ruisdael and Philips Koninck. Van der Neer's skies are an exquisite stop on the celestial journey of the history of painting, which a century earlier had been led by the blues of Patinir. The journey would then continue centuries later with James Arthur O'Connor, Carl Gustav Carus, Johan Christian Dahl, Ivan Aivazowsky and John Atkinson Grimshaw, among others.

An Asian connection is also present, as seen in the floating mountains/mountain-water/*shan shui* tradition of Chinese landscapes. This is apparent in the use of pigments that float and run throughout the works, as if the paint is trying to break free of the canvas. In *Montañas flotantes* (Floating Mountains) and *Los lados del cielo* (Sides of the Sky) the pictorial material overflows the canvas' borders.

My exhibition at The University Museum and Art Gallery in 2015 was also a tribute to the ancestors of the atmospheric perspective in Chinese Song dynasty painting, whose use of light resonates in their landscapes. In that exhibition, *Blue Expansive Landscape*, the common thread was the colour blue, which has been a consistent aspect of my career, from the expansive paintings, installations and photographic work to my abstract landscapes.

我在緬懷范．德．尼爾時，還聯想起與他同期的畫家，如雅各布．范．勒伊斯達爾和菲臘．科尼克。范．德．尼爾對天空的精彩詮釋可謂繪畫史上描繪天象旅程的精巧駐站。在上一個世紀，帕蒂尼爾以藍彩引領該風格潮流，繼往開來者還有詹姆士．阿塞．奧康奈爾、卡爾．古斯塔夫．卡魯斯、約翰．基斯汀．達爾、伊凡．艾瓦佐夫斯基、約翰．阿特金森．格里姆肖等。

新作系列中亦注入源於中國山水畫的亞洲元素。我刻意將顏料溢出畫布邊界，令其呈現飛浮奔馳的效果，就像顏料正力求擺脫畫布，這種情景在畫作《浮山》和《天空的邊》中尤為明顯。

我在2015年時於香港大學美術博物館舉辦「悠藍青境」展覽。當時利用筆觸向擅長透過光線來渲染風景中空氣感的宋代名畫家們致敬。藍色成為該展覽的主線，亦驟見於大型畫作、裝置及攝影作品和抽象風景畫，成爲我藝術生涯中標誌性的演繹。

我在香港先後兩次的展覽主題，均與我所關注的命題有關，亦因此詮釋了我的藝術：對物質的執著；對雲彩、宇宙、夜色的圖像處理、傳統中國畫的特徵，以及對法國抒情抽象風格的敬仰。兩次展覽之間的另一層連繫是聯覺，因為展出的繪畫作品都有意衝破既定的界限，並刻意與音樂等藝術媒介建立關係。

In both the earlier and current exhibition in Hong Kong there are similar concerns that define my art: an obsession over matter or substance; a specific pictorial treatment of clouds, the cosmos and night; aspects of traditional Chinese painting and my admiration for French lyrical abstraction. Synaesthesia is another link between the exhibitions, as the paintings are meant to reach beyond the medium to connect with other arts, especially music.

The concept of "expansion" is also a key factor in my paintings. By expanding the range of material pigments, I seek to engage with the public through multiple expressions of discourse where I have the opportunity to defend the continued validity of painting as a vibrant art form. Finally, the idea of expanded matter is present in my recent projects based in Asia. Taking this idea further, interacting with the public, I have staged live performances where I have expanded my abstract tri-dimensional landscapes. In these performances, and in my tribute to Aert van der Neer, I use the space to generate visual depth, an idea that exists both within and beyond the paintings.

Alberto Reguera

「延伸」這概念也是我的繪畫作品的重要元素。藉著擴充色彩範圍，我尋求透過多重藝術論述的表達與公眾互動，以證繪畫為一種持續充滿活力的藝術形式。由前所述，「延伸」的概念也出現在我近期在亞洲完成的創作項目。順延著這概念，我延伸抽象立體風景畫，為此進行現場表演，與觀眾互動，並藉著這藝術形式，利用畫內畫外的空間締造視覺深邃，向范・德・尼爾致敬。

艾拔圖・雷古拉

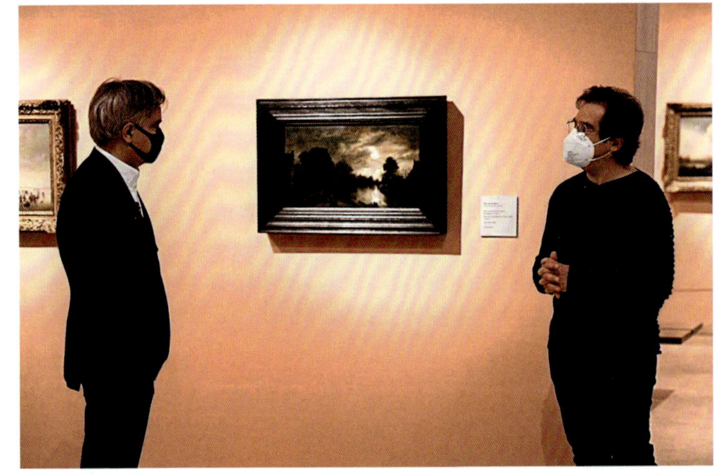

Guillermo Solana, Chief Curator and Artistic Director, Museo Thyssen-Bornemisza & Alberto Reguera with Aert van der Neer's painting *Moonlit Landscape*

提森-博內米薩國家博物館總館長及藝術總監基里爾莫．蘇蘭納和艾拔圖．雷古拉，中間為阿爾特．范．德．尼爾作品《皓月河旁徑》

A Conversation with Alberto Reguera

Guillermo Solana: The paintings in this exhibition were created in response to a work held in the Museo Thyssen, *Moonlit Landscape with a Road beside a Canal* by Aert van der Neer. This painting, and its dimensions, were the starting point for your work?

Alberto Reguera: Yes, that's right. Van der Neer's painting measures 35.6 x 65.5 x 7.5 cm, and I ordered stretchers for my canvases based on those proportions. In some cases I had to increase the size of the edge or the structure wouldn't have held up. One of my obsessions is the picture as object, the objectification of painting.

gs: It's noteworthy you should be interested in a small painting that not many have seen, or seen but possibly not remember.

ar: The first thing that caught my attention was how such a large landscape fit into such a compact space. I was, of course, also attracted by the clouds and how the moonlight filtered through. The shifting clouds and hues reminded me of one of my obsessions, the textures of sky with which I routinely work.

gs: Van der Neer specialised in nocturnal moonlit landscapes. You've painted many nocturnes, as well as landscapes in a dim dawn or dusk light.

ar: For many painters a nocturne can be a gateway to the imagination, a threshold between the visible and invisible. The fact that everything is vaguer and less defined allows the painter to use the palette to create nuances, which is a gateway to subtlety. To paint night, you need to be more subtle and imaginative.

與艾拔圖·雷古拉對話

蘇蘭納：這次展出的作品是為了回應提森博物館的藏品——阿爾特·范·德·尼爾的《皓月河旁徑》。我可以說這幅名作及其尺寸是你這次創作的起步點嗎？

雷古拉：對，《皓月河旁徑》的尺寸是35.6 x 65.5 x 7.5 厘米，我是根據這大小訂購畫布架的。但是有好幾幅需要大一點的邊框，否則支撐不起畫身。我追求畫即是物，並將這一理念具象化。

蘇蘭納：這幅面積小、又較少人看過或受關注的作品如此吸引著你，這本身就很有趣。

雷古拉：第一件引起我注意的事情是，如此遼闊的風景是如何裝進這麼狹窄的空間。另外，我當然也被畫裏的雲彩和穿透雲層的月光所吸引。那些在天空浮游的雲彩和色調讓我想起天空的質感——另一個我迷戀兼經常引入的繪畫題材。

蘇蘭納：范·德·尼爾擅長描繪月夜景色，你有很多作品也描繪夜景，還有晨光熹微或暮色蒼茫的風景。

雷古拉：對很多畫家來說，夜色是通向想像力的道路，是徘徊於若隱若現之間的臨界點。由於一切景物被雲山霧罩、朦朧不清，這允許畫家利用調色板描繪細節，開啟精妙之門。事實上，夜景要畫得好，畫家需要有著精湛的技法和豐富的想象力。

In my paintings night isn't black; it's better expressed in blue, especially Prussian blue. When gazing at the stars on a summer's night, you see a depth like a velvet fabric—you don't know where it begins or ends. Kandinsky said that blue is the most spiritual colour. The deeper the blue the more spiritual. It's a more intangible colour, perhaps more weightless than the others.

我不用黑色描繪夜景，而是使用藍彩，尤其是普魯斯藍。如果在夏夜仰望星空，你會看見天鵝絨一般的深邃，不知其起於何處，又將盡於何方。康丁斯基曾說，藍色是最有靈性的顏色，其色越深，越富靈性。它是無形的顏色，甚至乎比其它色彩都更為輕盈。

Clouds

gs: One of the elements that you often highlight in your paintings is clouds.

ar: Yes, clouds are the centrepiece of landscape painting, not just in the Dutch tradition. This is also the case, for example, in Chinese painting. The Chinese began with the concept that the cloud was a type of medial space between mountain and sky. Great importance was attached to the concept of the void. The void has its place in the picture through the representation of the condensation of water droplets in the form of a mountain. It's the idea of *shan shui* (water-mountain). For Chinese painters, a cloud is almost a demiurge that can establish those balances, the harmonies they need to create space between, above and below. Wang Wei, the Tang dynasty poet and painter, spoke of how clouds eventually give way to a clarity, a blue aura from which clouds and storms have disappeared.

Clouds are in constant fleeting motion, and every instant is unique because clouds are constantly being formed and transformed. This is why clouds represent time. In the West, after the Dutch, clouds became the primary feature of nineteenth-century landscape painting from the Romantics to the Impressionists. We might speak of those upward sweeping compositions, of how they give the impression that the clouds seem to want to

雲

蘇蘭納：雲是你的作品中經常强調的元素。

雷古拉：不錯，雲在風景畫裏是最引人矚目的，不僅在荷蘭的繪畫傳統中如此，在其他繪畫作品如中國畫中，也是不可或缺的。中國人認為，雲代表山與天之間的空間。「空」的概念十分重要。在構圖上「空」有其位，即呈現水凝為滴，以山為形，方成「山水」。對中國畫家來說，雲幾乎能造物，可以建立平衡，創造畫面高遠、深遠和平遠空間的和諧。唐代詩人畫家王維有詩云：「白雲回望合，青靄入看無」。

連綿起伏的浮雲變幻莫測，因此雲代表著時間。在西方，繼荷蘭黃金時代風景畫家之後，雲成為十九世紀浪漫派乃至印象派風景畫的重要特徵。當中向上橫掃的筆觸，予人一種亂雲彷彿要從畫面撲出來的錯覺，而另一方面又呈現著雲層緩緩地橫向飄遊。這一切的景象都好像是為了訴說大自然的故事。

leap from the picture, of how they progressively make a sequence of clouds in horizontal formats that, ultimately, are telling a story about nature.

Travel

gs: You've always had a special connection with Dutch landscape painting, and with the actual landscapes of the Netherlands.

ar: When I first travelled to Holland it was a bit like reencountering the aesthetic world of Castilian landscape painting: it is both above and below horizons, a very Rothkian world. And that influenced me greatly. This gave rise to a series of sketches that didn't materialise into paintings but were stored in my memory. I made mental sketches of my experience of the landscape at a particular moment, which later inspired a series of paintings.

During my trips to Holland in the 1990s, I was transfixed by its marvelous plains and infinite horizons. At the same time, I began to recognise those marvellous landscapes in the museums. I immediately fell in love with the landscapes of Dutch artists like Hendrick Avercamp, Pieter de Molijn, Jan van Goyen, Aelbert Cuyp, Philips Koninck and Jacob van Ruisdael, among others. I was also reading Paul Claudel, who masterly described Holland's ever changing skies. Claudel wrote about feeling a 'secret elasticity' as he walked across the land. My encounter with Dutch painting is a symbiosis between the landscape that I travelled across and the painted landscapes that I saw.

gs: Another trip you often talk about is one you made to Norway.

ar: I travelled to Norway in 1998, but I'd been imagining and painting Norwegian landscapes long before that. Let me ex-

旅程

蘇蘭納：你與荷蘭繪畫和荷蘭當地的風景結下不解之緣。

雷古拉：我初訪荷蘭時，猶如再次置身於西班牙卡斯蒂利亞風景畫的美學世界。那起起伏伏的地平線，像極羅斯克式的繪畫世界，就此啟發我創作了一系列畫稿。雖然最終沒有完成作品，但在腦海裏當刻對山光水色的感受已貯藏在記憶中，啟發往後創作的靈感。

二十世紀九十年代，我多次到訪荷蘭，總被那裏廣袤壯麗的平原和無盡伸展的地平線吸引，常看得入神。同時，我又注意到博物館裏那些偉大的風景畫作品，並愛上荷蘭風景畫家亨利克・阿維坎普、比得・迪・莫霖津、楊・范・戈因、艾伯特・克伊普、菲臘斯・科尼克、雅各布・范・勒伊斯達爾登等大師的作品。此外，我也閱讀法國詩人保羅・克洛岱爾的作品，他對荷蘭天空萬變景色的描寫十分精彩。他曾以「神秘的柔韌」來形容其行走在大地上的感受。我接觸的荷蘭繪畫，其實是旅途中所見的自然風光和風景畫的共生。

蘇蘭納：你經常提起的另一趟旅程就是到訪挪威。

雷古拉：1998年，我造訪挪威，但許久之前已幻想過和繪畫過那裏的風景。容許我解釋一下：在一次展覽中，我看到十九世紀瑞典

plain—at an exhibition I'd come across a nineteenth-century Swedish photographer, Axel Lindahl, who portrays the Norwegian landscape. His photographs show universes captured within mountains—rather like what Monet created from his trip to Norway. But interestingly, I was more intrigued by Lindahl's Norway than Monet's. So, two years before visiting Norway I was already painting these fjords because I'd been studying the photos. And when I started using pigment, I began tossing it on more vertically than horizontally, to create a sort of...

gs: Curtain?

ar: Yes, curtains of light. A fjord is like a natural cathedral. In 1998, Violette Heger-Hedløy, my gallerist at the time, encouraged me to visit Norway, and it was an amazing experience. I travelled in the Hurtigruten, which is a boat that takes you to the Lofoten Islands and stops at the fjords. In the boat—between sky, sea and land—was incredible. And the strange thing was that I started coming across some of the landscapes I'd already painted. At night I dreamed about those pictures in motion, incorporated into the landscape. As we travelled along, the horizon disappeared, sky and earth merged. I think that helped me to get over my complex about wanting to be a purely abstract painter and made me more receptive to landscapes. That trip was a great learning process.

And then came other trips: in 2006 I went to New Zealand because I wanted to see a divergent landscape. A natural world also located close to a pole, but much lusher. But when you discover a landscape that's so close to your own universe, is there anything your paint can really contribute? So, I ended up producing more photographs than paintings. Of course, when I use the camera I'm also painting, but painting with my eyes.

攝影師艾塞．蘭度拍下的挪威風光。他的照片呈現了封存在山巒中的世界，有點像莫奈到訪挪威之後所繪的風景畫。可是我對蘭度鏡頭下的挪威，比對莫奈所繪的挪威更感興趣。因此，在挪威之行的兩年前，我已著手研究蘭度的攝影，以峽灣之景入畫，並採用縱向而非橫向的著色手法，製造一種……

蘇蘭納：簾幕？

雷古拉：對，光簾的效果。峽灣宛如大自然的大教堂。在1998年，當時我的畫廊經理人維奧莉特．希嘉-赫特萊鼓勵我造訪挪威，這簡直是一趟奇妙的旅程！我搭乘海達路郵輪前往羅浮敦群島，船隻停經峽灣。在遊輪上，穿行於蒼穹、大海和陸地三者之間，實在妙不可言。最不可思議的是，我眼前開始出現從前畫過的風景，晚上更夢到我所畫的圖像一邊變動，一邊與真實的風景結合。船隻航行之際，地平線亦告消失，最後天地相接。那次經歷使我徹底打消我對成為純抽象畫家的情結，也令我更加接受風景畫。這趟旅程實在使我獲益匪淺！

還有更多的旅行值得一提：2006年，我造訪紐西蘭，想看看當地的特殊地貌。紐西蘭的自然風貌非常接近地球之極，卻草木蔥鬱。當你發現一個所視之景與自己的小天地如此接近時，畫筆有何用武之地？結果我在該地所拍攝的相片比繪畫更多。當然，我在使用相機時也是在繪畫，只不過以目代筆罷了。

Music

ar: There's a particular subject also related to travel—the issue of fleeing. I've always painted pictures in flight.

gs: One of your paintings is even titled *Paysage en fuite*.

ar: It's like everything is in motion. Everything is also related to the clouds, which look as though they want to float away from the picture. I'm interested in that sort of flight, too.

gs: I've heard you speak about the analogy with the fugue as a form of music. One voice begins and the second voice follows behind, and then maybe a third or a fourth.

ar: That's right, they're layers, which in the end are superimposed in a polyphony. Let's say that, if travel is an element of inspiration, then music is another crucial aspect. I nearly always paint while listening to music, because music creates a climate, an atmosphere that helps get my juices flowing in the studio. There's a power in synaesthesia, of painting the topography of music, speaking of my textures, of converting sound into colour. Like in the experiments of Kandinsky, Scriabin, Mark Tobey and John Cage. One of my paintings, *Vibrations of Mozart*, was shown at UMAG in Hong Kong in 2015, and I've painted Telemann pictures, Mendelssohn pictures, Grieg pictures, Sibelius pictures, Satie pictures . . . I also collaborated with the Dutch contemporary musician Bart Spaan: he drew inspiration from my paintings when composing musical works, and I drew inspiration from his music to paint.

gs: You usually mention Haydn as your favourite musician.

ar: He's the great master. He transmits a sort of vibration of life, from his *Sturm und Drang* symphonies—which are proto-Romantic but powerfully Romantic—to the London symphonies.

音樂

雷古拉：還有一個特別的主題也與旅行有關，就是「逃離」這個概念。我總是繪畫與逃走有關的圖像。

蘇蘭納：你甚至有一幅畫名為《逃走的風景》。

雷古拉：畫中一切都似乎在游動，所有事物均與天上的雲有關，看起來好像要從畫面浮游而去。我對「逃離」這一主題也感興趣。

蘇蘭納：我聽說你曾用復調音樂體裁的賦格曲作比喻，從第一個聲部開始，漸次疊加第二、第三和第四聲部。

雷古拉：正是如此。是有層次感的複疊而成的複調音樂。這樣說吧，若旅行是靈感的元素，那麼音樂便是另一種重要的靈感泉源。我幾乎總是一邊繪畫一邊聽音樂，因為音樂能製造一種氣氛，一種推動我在畫室內發揮創意的力量。聯覺的力量強大，容許我繪出音樂的形狀。就畫作的肌理而言，可把聲音轉化成顏色，就像康定斯基、史克里亞賓、馬克．托比、約翰．基治等人做的試驗。2015年，我有一幅名為《莫札特的震動》的作品在港大美術博物館展出。此外，我又畫過泰勒曼、孟德爾遜、葛里格、西貝流士、薩堤等大師的音樂。我也曾與荷蘭當代音樂家伯德．史班合作，他在創作音樂作品時從我的畫中得到啟發，而我從他的音樂中也得以汲取作畫靈感。

I like to paint the sun's brightness listening to Haydn's music. To me—since I live between Paris and Madrid—it brings to mind a Sunday morning in Paris, a day where the sky isn't overcast, a bright morning. Haydn helps me create pictorial melodies and he's also accompanied me during my performances in front of an audience, like those I recently staged in China.

Materials

gs: You've always worked within the medium of painting, experimenting with it.

ar: I think this obsession with the materiality of painting comes from childhood. I was born in Castile surrounded by the texture of seas of wheat. And as a child I remember gazing at flaking walls (when you're little, a wall can be a universe) and that characteristic graffiti of the city of Segovia. That's probably where my obsession for painting comes from, for creating layers and scratching. Later on, when I was twenty, I began visiting museums and discovered Max Ernst's grattages. Taking away material only to put it back, deconstructing to construct. And after all those layers and scratching away, how do you finish? Those layers, those strata like raw flesh, all of it needs to be covered; let's say it needs glazing over. How could it be made more subtle? So, I began experimenting with pigment.

gs: Powdered pigment as a glaze.

ar: Pigment is a material that both traps and gives off light; it has that dual ability. But to create the glaze you have to apply it over a freshly painted surface. With the picture set at an angle, I started tossing it on, as if I were 'sowing' the canvas. Perhaps, though I'm not actually aware of it at the time, I could imagine this act as a

蘇蘭納：你經常提及你最喜愛的音樂家海頓。

雷古拉：海頓是一位偉大的音樂家，他向倫敦交響樂團呈奏《狂飆運動》交響樂，表彰內心感情的衝突。該作誕生於浪漫主義萌芽時期，具有濃厚的浪漫主義風格特徵。我繪畫那絢爛的太陽時，總愛聽著海頓的音樂。由於我在巴黎和馬德里都有住所，海頓的音樂令我想起星期日巴黎的朝暉，萬里無雲，天色澄霽。海頓的音樂啟發我創作如旋律般的畫作，亦陪伴我在觀眾面前演出，我近期在中國的表演便為一例。

物料

蘇蘭納：你一直用顏料創作，並不斷進行實驗。

雷古拉：我對繪畫顏料的執迷始於童年的經歷。我在西班牙卡斯蒂利亞出生，到處都是麥田。我還記得小時候喜歡盯著油漆斑駁的牆壁(對小朋友來說，一堵牆可能已經代表一切)，還有塞哥維亞城裏特有的塗鴉。這可能解釋到我為何醉心於繪畫，因為它能夠製造層次感和刮痕。我二十歲開始參觀博物館時，便發現馬克思．恩斯特的刮擦法畫作，就是把油畫顏料除去，目的是為了重新塗於畫布上，即將之解體後重組。這種把顏料反覆層疊後又刮走的做法，難免有人會問我是如何完成畫作。那層層的顏料形似活生

painterly gesture: sprinkling pigment over fresh paint to create a series of textures, of glazes the light can filter through. I want the layers beneath to be seen, and for all of them to be unified by a coating of pigment which might be, for example, Prussian blue or bright yellow. In addition, when I toss the pigment in a particular direction, I try to imitate the effect of light illuminating the landscape. If I toss it from one of the ends of the picture, the relief of the landscape appears to be lit by the raking light of dawn or dusk. I can also recreate the intensity of midday light in Castile if I apply the pigment standing in front of the work. And if I do so from several sides, I can create other textures.

Cosmic

ar: Let's say that the pigment progressively creates the picture for you, it weaves it bit by bit. And a slightly cosmic, mysterious side appears . . . what the great poet Andrée Chedid called *l'étoffe de l'univers*—the matter, the fabric of the universe.

I believe that my vision of landscapes goes beyond the earth's surface. I have a kind of transverse idea of painting; I can paint seas of wheat, then the sky, the clouds, first the lowest and then the highest. You go up up up into the atmosphere, as far as the stratosphere, and nearer and nearer the cosmos. I have many pictures that are quite cosmic. This structure of microscopic elements forming pigment, and of pigments that come together in a sort of tapestry, becomes the tapestry of the universe. In other words, there's an extremely terrestrial side to my painting, but there's also a very cosmic side, and sometimes my painting shifts from one extreme to another.

生的血肉，須被皮膚包裹覆上的組織層般，必須掩蓋好，就如畫作需要塗上一層光油。我應當如何細緻地處理這種創作方法呢？結果，我對顏料進行各項實驗。

蘇蘭納：色粉如釉料。

雷古拉：顏料具備兩種功能，既吸光也放光。但如果要取得釉面的效果，便必須把顏料塗在剛上色的表面上。我把畫布設置於一個角度，然後灑上顏料，就仿佛在畫布上「播種」一樣。也許我當時並不為意，回想起來，我可以把這種行為想像成一種繪畫的姿態：把顏料揮灑在未乾的顏料上，製造一層層恍如釉面的肌理，令光線可穿透顏料。我希望那些底層的顏料受到注視，並與普魯斯藍或鮮黃色等顏料塗層共冶一爐。此外，當我朝著某方向灑色時，我嘗試模仿光線照耀風景的效果。如果從畫的一端投擲顏料，那度黎明或黃昏的斜照便彷佛燃亮了這片風景的輪廓。當我站在畫作的正前方灑色，便可重現卡斯蒂利亞的正午強光。若我在各方位都重施故技，便可製造出迥然不同的肌理。

宇宙

雷古拉：假設顏料漸進式地編織圖像，勾勒出神秘的宇宙之象......就正如偉大詩人安德烈・佘蒂筆下的《宇宙的織物》：物質，為宇宙的織物。

gs: I recall a newspaper article about a cloud of gas 3,500 light years long that stretches across the entire Milky Way. It reminded me of your painting, because it has an iridescence whose brightness shifts greatly.

ar: Today we're becoming accustomed to recognizing geographies beyond our planet, of the Moon or Mars, which used to be unusual and now can be seen on Instagram. We're starting to become familiar with images, for instance, of a storm on Jupiter that's larger than the entire Earth.

And it's marvelous to think about how the universe generates a geometry that man wouldn't be capable of creating. For example, Saturn's rings are actually elements of dust aligned in distinct patterns of colour. They're perfectly aligned around something else that attracts them. Pure geometric painting.

gs: Your painting brings to mind those processes.

ar: Yes, let's call them cosmic processes. I also think about dark matter, which is like extrapolating the world of night towards the cosmos. You're looking at a cluster and deep down you don't know if it's a cloud or an enormous nebula. And in the middle is dark matter.

Viewpoint

ar: I've worked with metal pigments for many years: copper, silver, iridium pigments. Their iridescence changes depending on the spectator's viewpoint. Based on the direction of the light, the same pigment can appear dark or shiny, and then I see different pictures.

我相信我對風景的視野超越了地球表面，有一種橫向的繪畫觀念。我可以繪畫廣闊的麥田、天空、雲朵，先由畫面最低處畫起，繼而向最高處延伸，到達大氣平流層，直至接近宇宙。我的作品多與宇宙有關。這種微元素的結構凝聚成顏料，顏料又組成某種掛毯，成為宇宙的織物。換然之，我的畫作有屬於地的一面，也有屬於天的一面，有時則遊走於天地之間。

蘇蘭納：我曾經在報章上讀過，有一團三千五百光年長的氣體雲，橫跨整個銀河系，就像虹彩般的亮度變幻無常，這使我想起你的畫作。

雷古拉：我們現在習慣看到地球以外的天體，甚至能認出月球和火星表面的地形。這些景象以往都是難得一見的，如今卻能在社交媒體上看到。我們也開始熟悉天體圖像。例如，能夠看見木星表面刮起的一場風暴，覆蓋面積比整個地球還要大的影像，如今對人們而言已屢見不鮮。

一想起宇宙衍生人類無法創造的幾何體便覺得神奇。例如土星環其實是排列成不同著色圖案的塵土，而這些微塵又完美地環繞著牽引它們的物質，形成純幾何繪畫。

蘇蘭納：你的畫正好讓人聯想起這些過程。

雷古拉：對，我們尚且稱之為宇宙過程。我也想過暗物質，就好像把黑夜世界推向宇宙。你正看著一個星團，心底裏不肯定它到

These effects that change depending on viewpoint led me to think about involving the audience. Making them realize that, depending on where they stand, they can create their own version of the artwork. Being receptive to that variation.

gs: This interaction with spectators requires a three-dimensional picture, doesn't it?

ar: There's always been a natural process of applying layers in my paintings. Lucio Muñoz used to say to me: "Your painting process is like a pendulum. Sometimes there are lots of layers and in other pictures it's flat, very flat". Pictures that end up overflowing with layers are ultimately not just an imagined and abstract landscape; they're also objects. Canogar also remarked: "You're objectifying a landscape".

Painting as object

gs: Am I correct in suggesting that the dimensions of your paintings have grown over time?

ar: Painting is both a window through which our gaze must enter and an object that comes to meet us—which leaves the wall and interrogates us. An object that asks the spectator to move around the picture, to generate different pictures.

I had progressively thickened the canvas stretcher and one day, quite spontaneously and unintentionally—as these pictures were now so thick they could rest on the floor, and there wasn't much space left in the studio—I stood a picture on the floor. At that precise moment someone called and I left the painting. When I came back I suddenly realised that the painting could be independent from the wall. Then I added another picture

底是片雲朵，還是巨型星雲。夾雜其中的則是暗物質。

視點

雷古拉：多年來我已經開始使用銅、銀、銤等顏料。這些金屬顏料所產生的虹彩現象隨著觀者對物體表面的角度變動而令其色彩也隨之改變。同一顏料會根據光線的方向顯得時暗時亮，因而成像各異。

這種因觀點而異的效果，讓我希望觀者參與創作，令他們意識到，他們可透過決定站立的位置，為作品創造不同的版本，從而感受到作品的演化。

蘇蘭納：即是說，與觀眾互動時需要立體畫作，是這樣嗎？

雷古拉：反覆塗上顏料是我作畫最理所當然的過程。另一位西班牙藝術家盧斯奧．莫尼奧對我說過：「你作畫的過程像鐘擺，有些作品層層堆疊，另一些卻平坦，非常平坦。」那些層層疊疊的畫面，彷彿不勝負荷，它們終究不僅是幻想或抽象的風景，亦是物件。西班牙抽象藝術家卡諾家曾這樣說：「你將風景物化了。」

畫亦是物

蘇蘭納：你的畫作的尺寸隨著年月漸長而延伸，我這樣說對嗎？

to that picture to see what would happen—placing a group of pictures of different sizes directly on the floor. I remember someone seeing the assemblage and saying to me: "it's a family of paintings, like an abstraction of the Meninas".

Joselina Cruz, curator of the 2008 Singapore Biennial, wrote that it was like shattering the historical divergencies between painting and installation. And curiously, that process also arose at a time when I was expanding into Asia, which was in 2007. At the time I was into creating atmospheres with volume, brushstrokes with volume, and creating a picture with volume. Inviting spectators to walk around and create their own field of vision, to build their own picture. So, there's a logical process right from the start, isn't there? Of creating those textures until the material overflows and ends up turning into an independent object.

Performance

gs: And from objects to performance art. Tell me about when and how you made that leap.

ar: Around 2007, I started projecting my paintings into space, first horizontally, through a series of installations that involved placing paintings on the floor. But at the same time, while exploring my works' relationship with space, I began expanding canvases into three-dimensional pictures, which I placed on a variety of supports. For example, on a blank canvas or wall. I expanded the painting across those surfaces. It was as if the work from which the colours sprang were actually spewing out the material.

雷古拉：畫作既是我們的視窗，也是迎接觀者的物件——脫離牆壁向我們審問。它是一件要求觀者繞著來看，從而產生不同畫面的物件。

我在畫布上用顏料層層厚塗。有一天，我見畫作上的顏料實在太厚，於是打算把畫作躺平，卻發現工作室空間不足，因此不以爲然地把畫作豎立於地上。就在那一刻，電話響起，當我接聽完電話後回來，驀然發現一幅畫原來可以完全脫離於牆壁。於是我把另一幅畫置於地上，就在剛才那幅畫的旁邊，然後與其它組件一起在地上佈置，看看效果如何。記得有一位看過這個裝置的人對我說：「這是一套畫，像是把委拉斯蓋茲的《宮女》化成抽象畫」。

2008年，新加坡雙年展的策展人谷口瑪麗亞，評價此創作方式就如打破了繪畫與裝置藝術之間歷來的分野。有趣的是，這個創作手法發生於2007年，剛好是我開始前往亞洲發展的時候。當時我沉醉於以空間深度來塑造氣氛、筆觸和圖像，邀請觀眾繞著畫作四處走動，以建立獨特的視覺，製造屬於自己的圖象。這個創作過程——運用重叠交錯的顏料肌理溢出畫布以外的作法，並最終製成獨立作品——從一開始不就很順理成章嗎？

gs: The picture spewed out its own colour, spread around its own paint . . .

ar: Yes, because, like I was saying earlier, there's an entire universe in here. It's like I'd placed a cloud into a crate, an almost transparent box, and then pierced the cloud through the crate in order to expose the cloud's innards. I wanted to release a bit of that material; expel it to give rise to a series of paths, routes that the material could follow. On a wall you can't discern the difference between the finite and the infinite. You can on canvas. But the debate about the support remains. So, not wanting to get stuck in a rut, the next step for me around 2010 was to install a three-dimensional picture on the wall and then expand it in front of an audience. Invite the public to witness the action, in which the gesture is more important than the result. So, what I went on to do was to create that expansion in front of an audience, as if the substance, its very life force, were leaking out.

I remember one particular performance at the Hay Festival in Segovia in 2019, in front of 400 or 500 people. There was no preconceived idea or preliminary sketch of what was going to happen because I thought the most intense and exciting aspect of the performance was for it to emerge organically, while everyone was listening to the music. And on top of that there was a very good chance it might rain. When I began, the people seemed restless . . . some of the time I couldn't even look up because the audience was so large. Some of their initial restlessness was because I began extremely slowly; I always start slowly to get my bearings. After I relax a bit and start feeling more comfortable, I usually get so carried away that I become the brush.

There's a painting by Morris Louis that the artist created without ever touching the surface; he poured on the paint and controlled its flow by tipping the canvas in various directions to

表演藝術

蘇蘭納：從畫體到表演藝術，請告訴我是什麼驅使你跨出這一步。

雷古拉：大約在2007年，我開始將畫作投射於空間。起初透過一系列置於地上的裝置藝術把畫面橫向伸延。但在探索自身作品與空間關係的同時，我亦把畫布放在不同的支撐體上，以便延展畫布製造三維畫體。例如我在空白的畫布或牆壁上揮動顏料、擴展成一幅恰似流光溢彩的作品。

蘇蘭納：這幅畫色彩飛騰、彩花四濺。

雷古拉：對，就像我剛才說的，作品裏潛藏著整個宇宙：就像我把雲朵套入一個近乎透明的箱子裏，然後從箱外把雲朵刺穿，以表露出雲朵的內蘊。我想解放部分物料，將其放逐後，使之走出不同的路徑。在牆壁上，你無法分辨出有盡與無盡的分別，在畫布上卻可以。當然，有關支撐體的爭論從未停止。為免墨守成規，我在2010年前後決定邁進一步，把一幅立體畫安置在牆上，然後在觀眾面前為其延伸。我認為邀請公眾見證著創作過程的舉動，比起完成作品更為重要。所以我在觀眾面前作畫並延展畫作，務求呈現如物質那種活力四射的狀態。

記得在2019年，我參加了塞哥維亞的海伊文學藝術節，其中的一場表演有四五百位觀衆。我對這場演出事前完全沒有構思，亦沒有準備初稿，因為我認為表演藝術最刺

create images. Well, my form of performance is similar, except for that it's done in front of an audience, and there's a time limit. The body is crucial—specifically the body's movements, which brings us to the intersection with the other arts, like dance, because you move closer and then farther away, almost dancing through the picture.

gs: That reminds me a little of the performances of Robert Rauschenberg and Yves Klein.

ar: In expansions of this kind, both in public and private, my commitment is not only to interact with the spectator, but to create a painting's intangible aspects—that which surrounds it like an aura. In other words, the painting occupies more space than we give it physically. The vibrations, or its aura, are what I set out to materialise through this form of upward spilling or throwing.

My purpose is to see how painting can broaden paths and stress the validity of contemporary art. That is, many things can be managed with a classical painting, or a flat painting. A flat painting can expand and then go back into place. For example, one of my paintings is now in an exhibition in Beijing; at a specific moment that work became detached from its expansion. And maybe in a couple of years that same painting . . .

gs: Will give rise to other expansions.

ar: That same painting will have several lives. And not only in disciplines like painting, sculpture and installation, but also in those that go beyond the plastic arts—to music as an instrument of synaesthesia, dance and poetry. You can be inspired by someone reciting a poem and then paint. And that can be quite interesting, too.

激且有張力的，是即興和自發……再加上大家又可以同時聽音樂、又要面對下雨的不確定性。當我表演時，觀衆顯得有點躁動。另外，由於觀眾人數眾多，有時我甚至無法抬頭。最初觀衆不安的情緒是由於在表演開始時，我的進度非常緩慢；我總是慢慢起步以熟習環境。在我稍微放鬆、逐漸進入狀態後便遺物忘形，將自己化為畫筆。

藝術家莫里斯·路易斯曾在從未觸碰過畫布表面的情況下繪畫過一幅畫；他在畫布上倒進顏料，再調整畫架的斜度和方向來控制好顏料的流動而成像。其實我的表演形式與此類近，只不過我的創作是在觀眾面前進行，所以有時間限制。身體動作至關重要——尤其是行坐舉止——它把我們帶到不同藝術形式的交匯點，例如舞蹈，因為移動身體時與畫作的距離時遠時近，猶如在畫中翩翩起舞。

蘇蘭納：這使我想起羅伯特·勞森伯格和伊夫·克萊恩的表演藝術。

雷古拉：無論是公開或私下創作，為了承傳「延伸」的創作理念，我不僅積極與觀眾互動，亦創造繪畫的無形體——一種圍繞畫作的氛圍。換句話說，畫作實際佔據的空間比我們給予的尺寸體積來得多。透過朝上揮灑的動態，實現我一直追求的震顫和氛圍。

我旨在探索繪畫現今的發展動向，並足証繪畫在當代藝術中的效力。也就是說，古典繪

I remember in the performance I did at the Hay Festival, Ángela Segovia and Antonio Lucas went on stage after me to recite their poems while my painting was still there, drying. The audience's attention was on the poets when Antonio Lucas stopped and said: "And there's the painter, shyly collecting his pots and putting on the lids". I mean, when all the excitement is over you still have to clean up your pots so that the paint doesn't dry out; it brings you back to reality. Nor should you be afraid of rain, thunder or lightning when you're about to perform an expansive painting. If you're admiring the atmospheric elements contained within a picture, inside of a picture . . . what's there to be scared of? . . . having already marked up a wall to create an as yet unknown scene, are you really going to be scared off by a little rain? The rain might even help spread around the paint. The great landscape painters knew they were taking risks when they ventured beyond their studios. One should always be prepared to face such risks.

Guillermo Solana, Chief Curator and Artistic Director, Museo Thyssen-Bornemisza & Alberto Reguera

畫或平面畫可締造各種可能。一幅平面畫經延伸之後，可重回昔日狀態。例如一幅現正在北京展出的作品，在某個特定時刻它脫離了延展的狀態。可能在兩年後，這幅畫……

蘇蘭納：會延展出其它作品。

雷古拉：同一幅畫將有好幾代生命。不受繪畫、雕塑、裝置藝術等媒介所限，畫作可跨越造型藝術，把音樂、舞蹈或詩歌化成聯覺的工具。就如你可受詩歌朗誦啟發而繪畫一樣，實在相當有趣。

我記得在海伊文學藝術節中，西班牙詩人安琪娜．塞哥維亞和安東尼奧．盧卡斯在我演出後上台朗誦詩作。當時我的畫還未乾透，觀眾的注意力集中在兩位詩人身上，直至盧卡斯突然停止朗誦道：「還有這位畫家，正羞澀地收拾顏料，蓋上瓶蓋」。我的意思是，當興奮過後，還是要收拾顏料，蓋好瓶子，以防顏料乾掉，就這樣將人送返現實。此外，在即興表演創作延展畫時，也無須擔心下雨或行雷閃電。既然你如此欣賞畫中的氣象元素，那麼還有什麼好顧慮呢？演出前已為未知的風景在展覽牆上預留了空間，下雨這等小事又何懼之有？雨水反而還能有助顏料散開。風景畫大師們在步出畫室的一刻，便知道要承受未知的風險。我們創作藝術應時刻保持著冒險的精神。

基里爾莫．蘇蘭納（提森-博內米薩國家博物館總館長及藝術總監）和艾拔圖．雷古拉

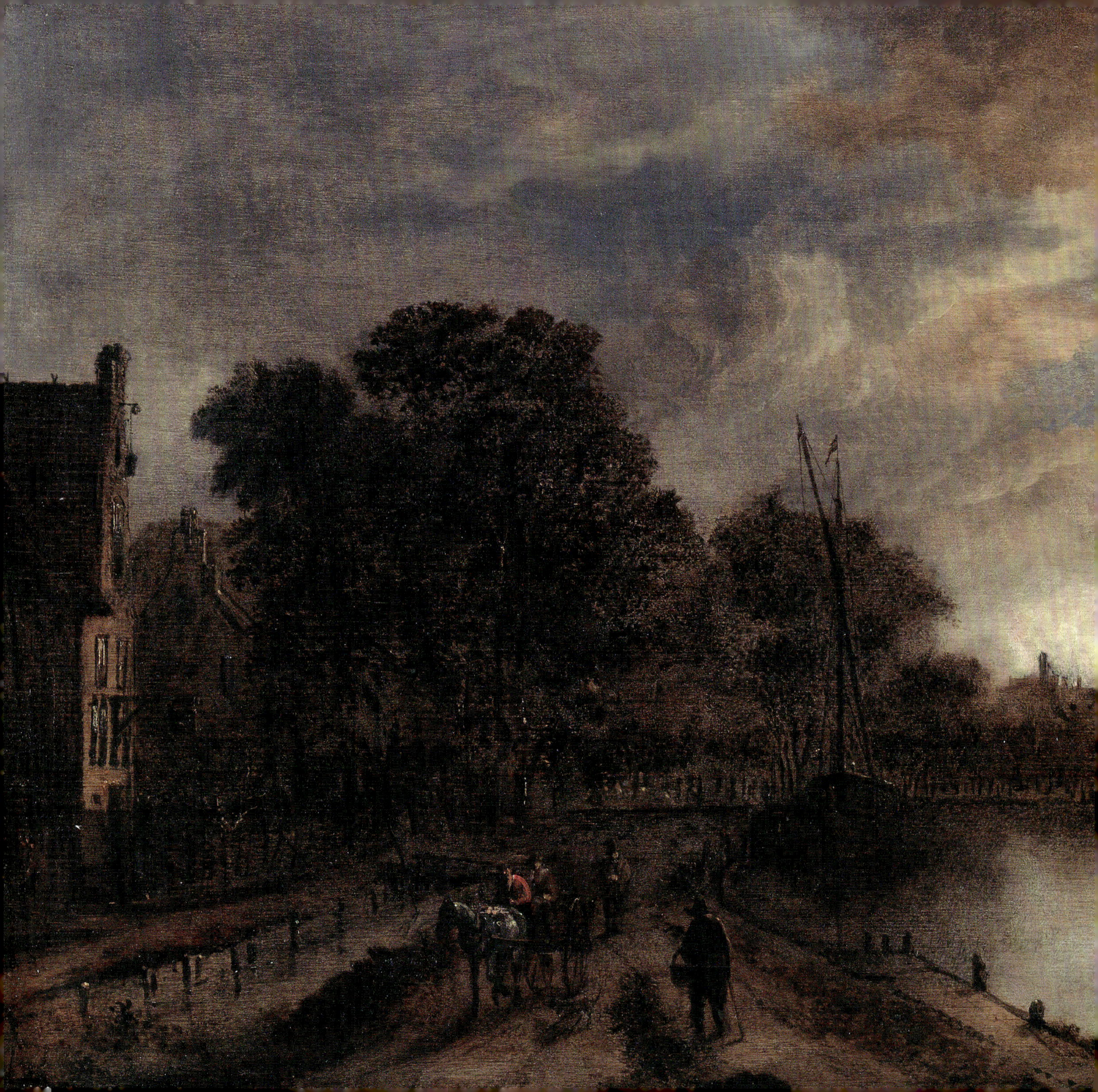

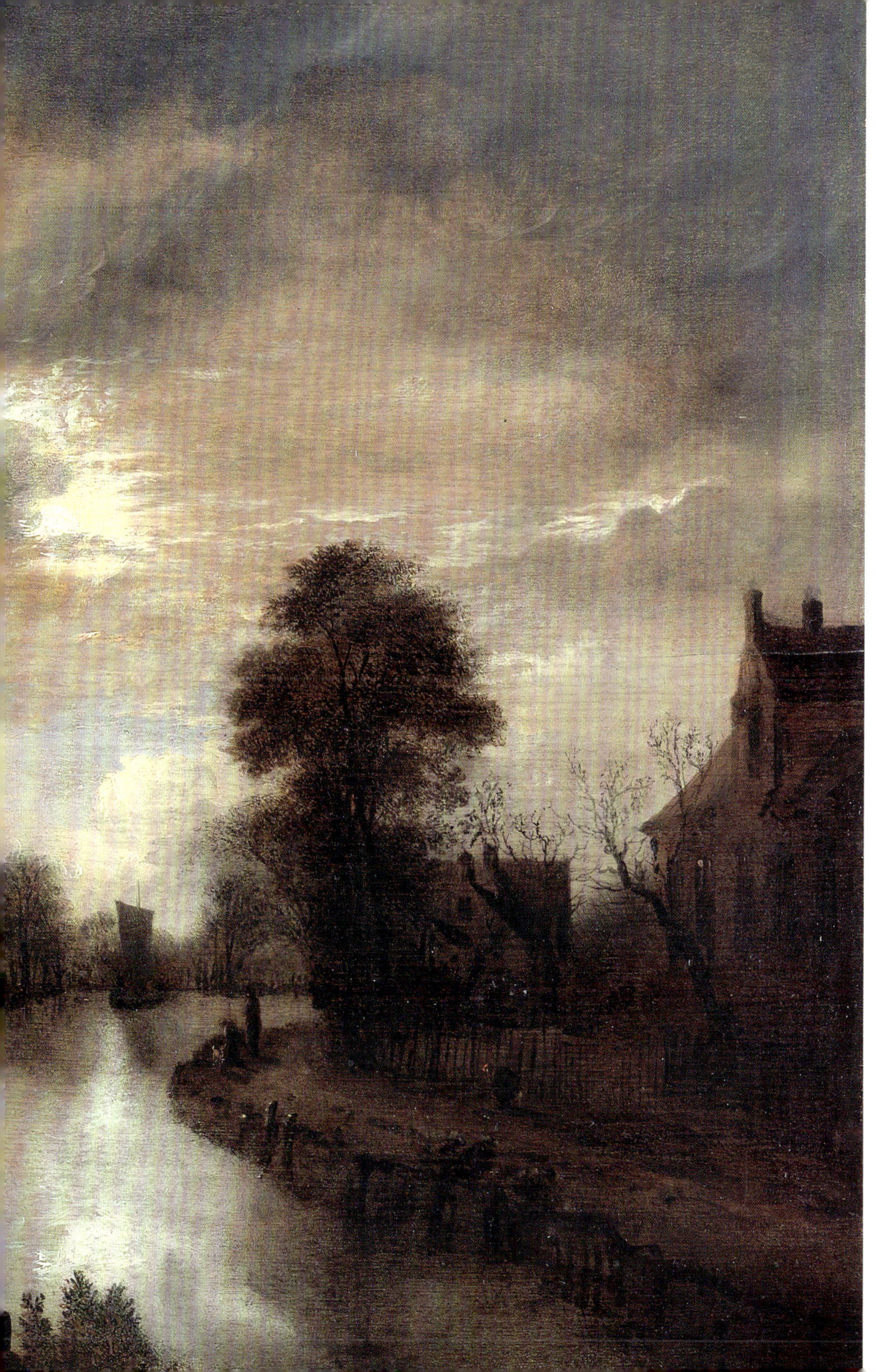

Moonlit Landscape with a Road beside a Canal (ca. 1645–50) Aert van der Neer

皓月河旁徑（約1645–50 年）
阿爾特 · 范 · 德 · 尼爾

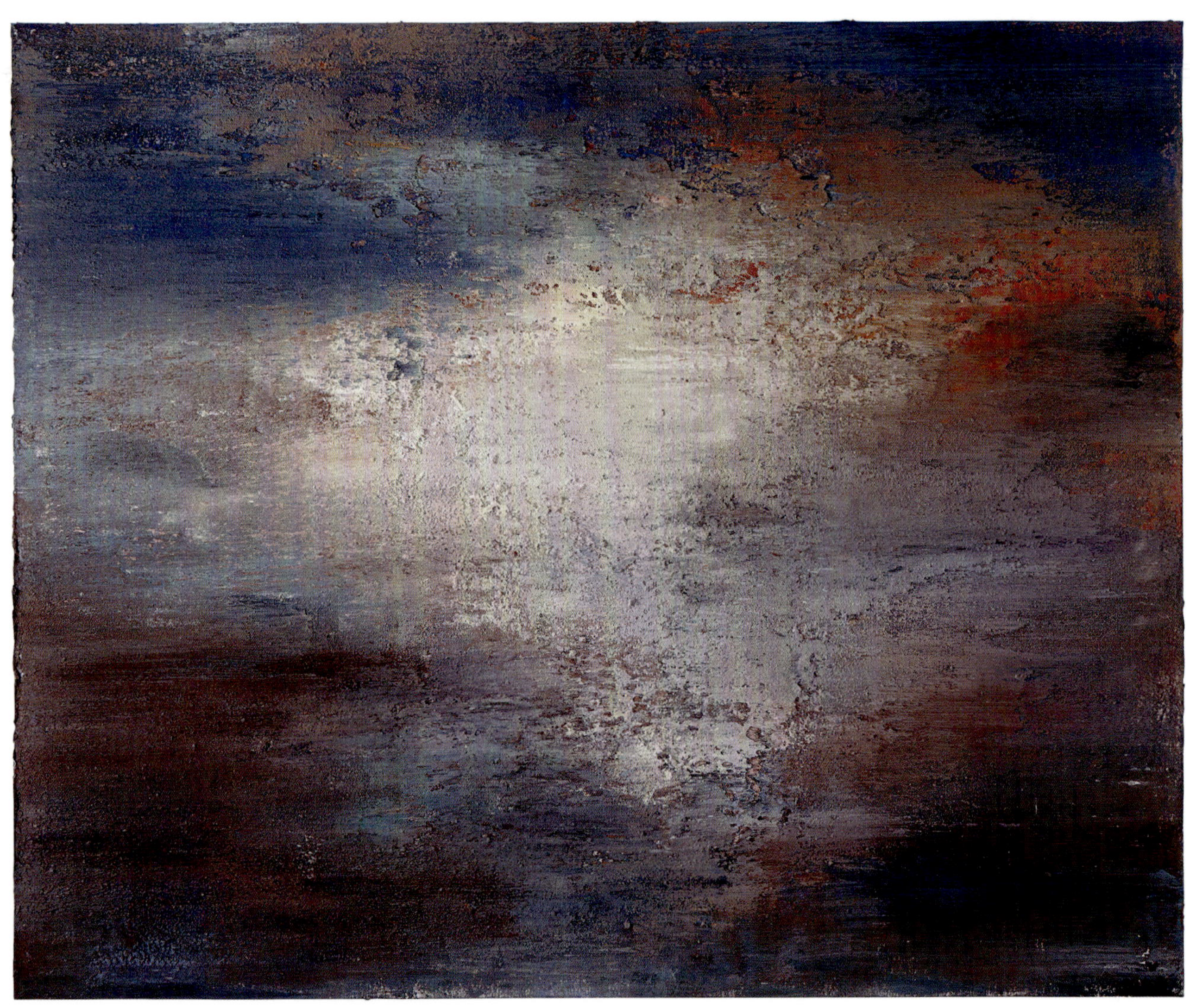

Illuminated Night 亮夜

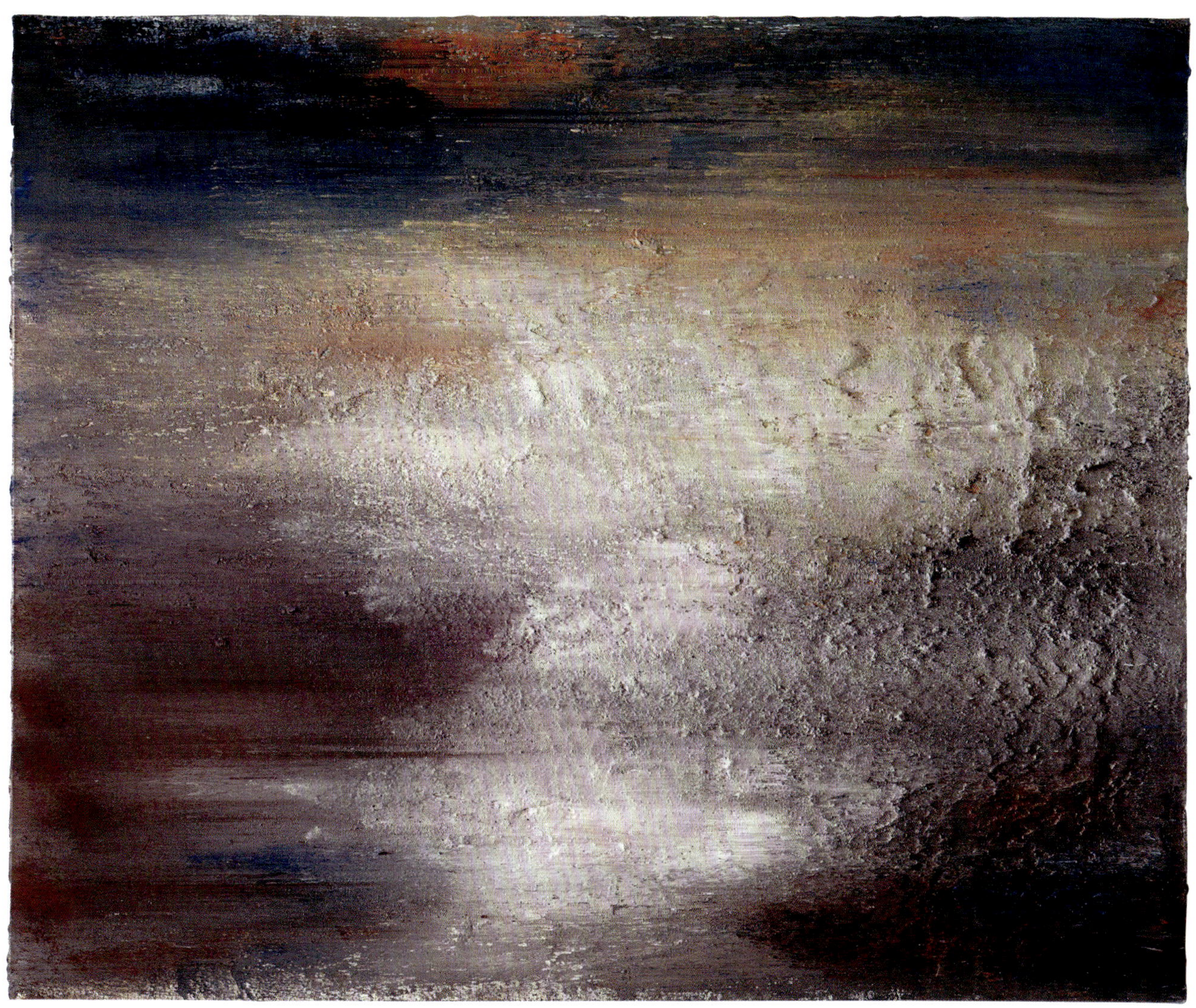

Immense Sky, Distant Horizon 曠天遠地

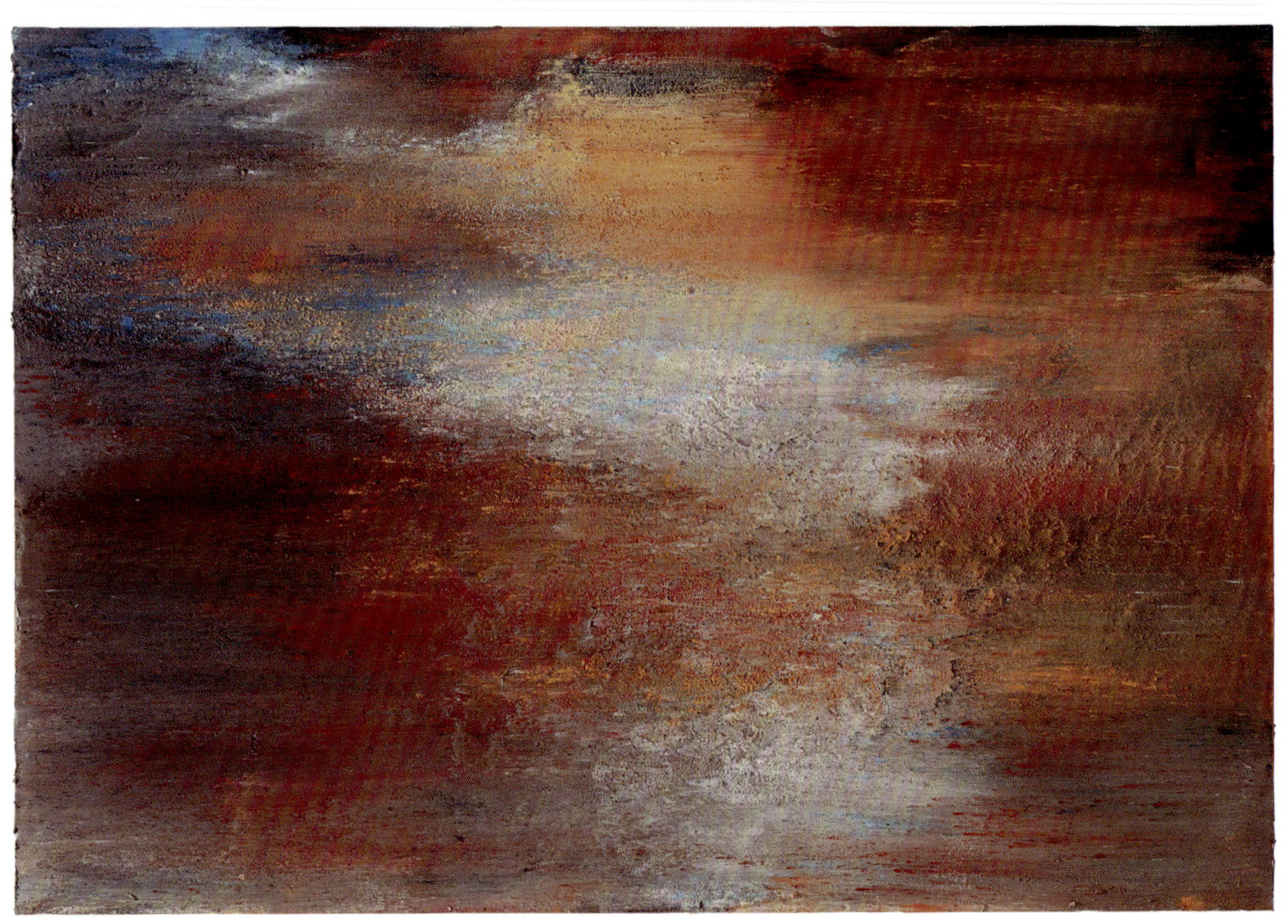

Lighting Routes 照亮路徑

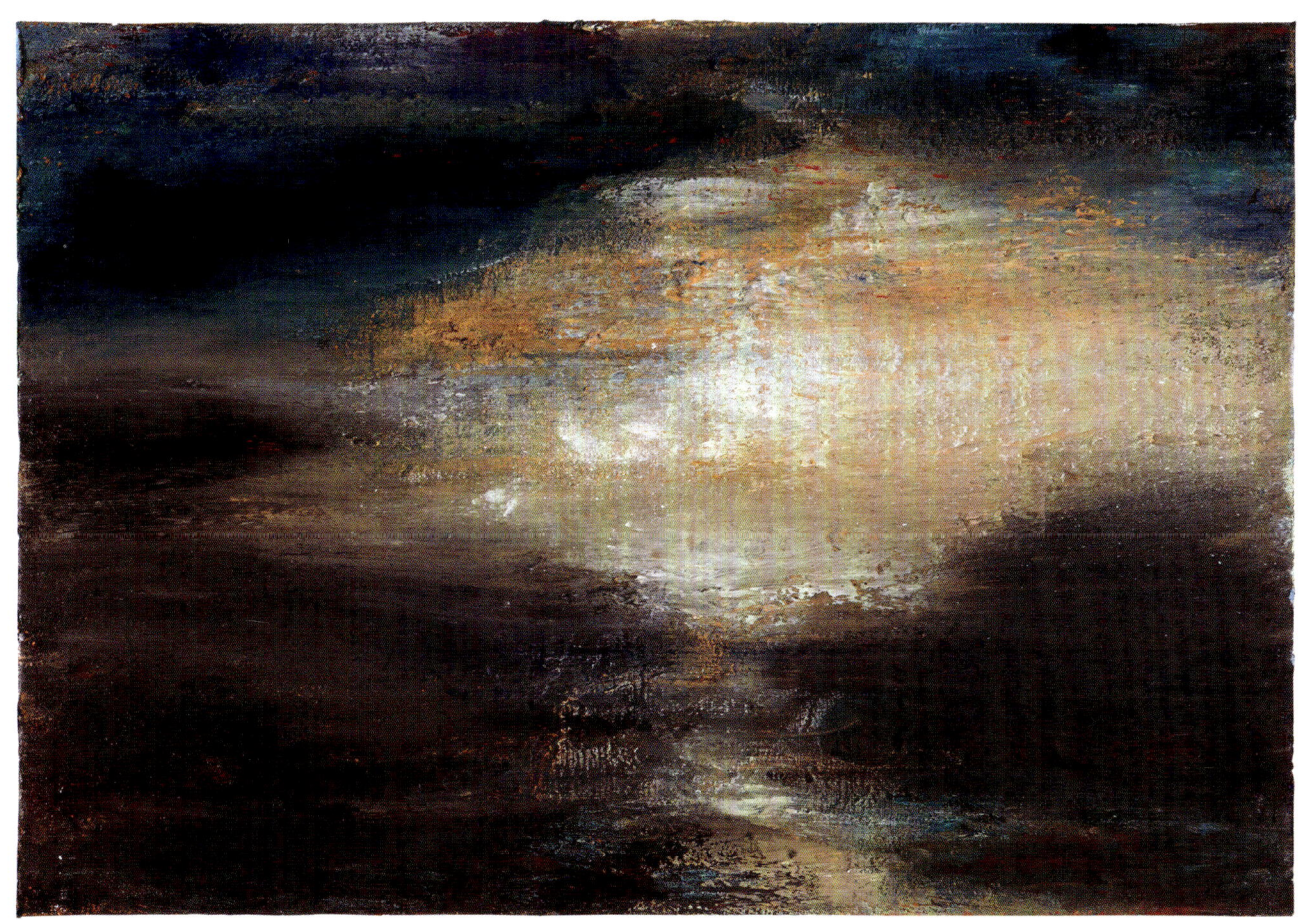

Night Glare 夜裏光焰

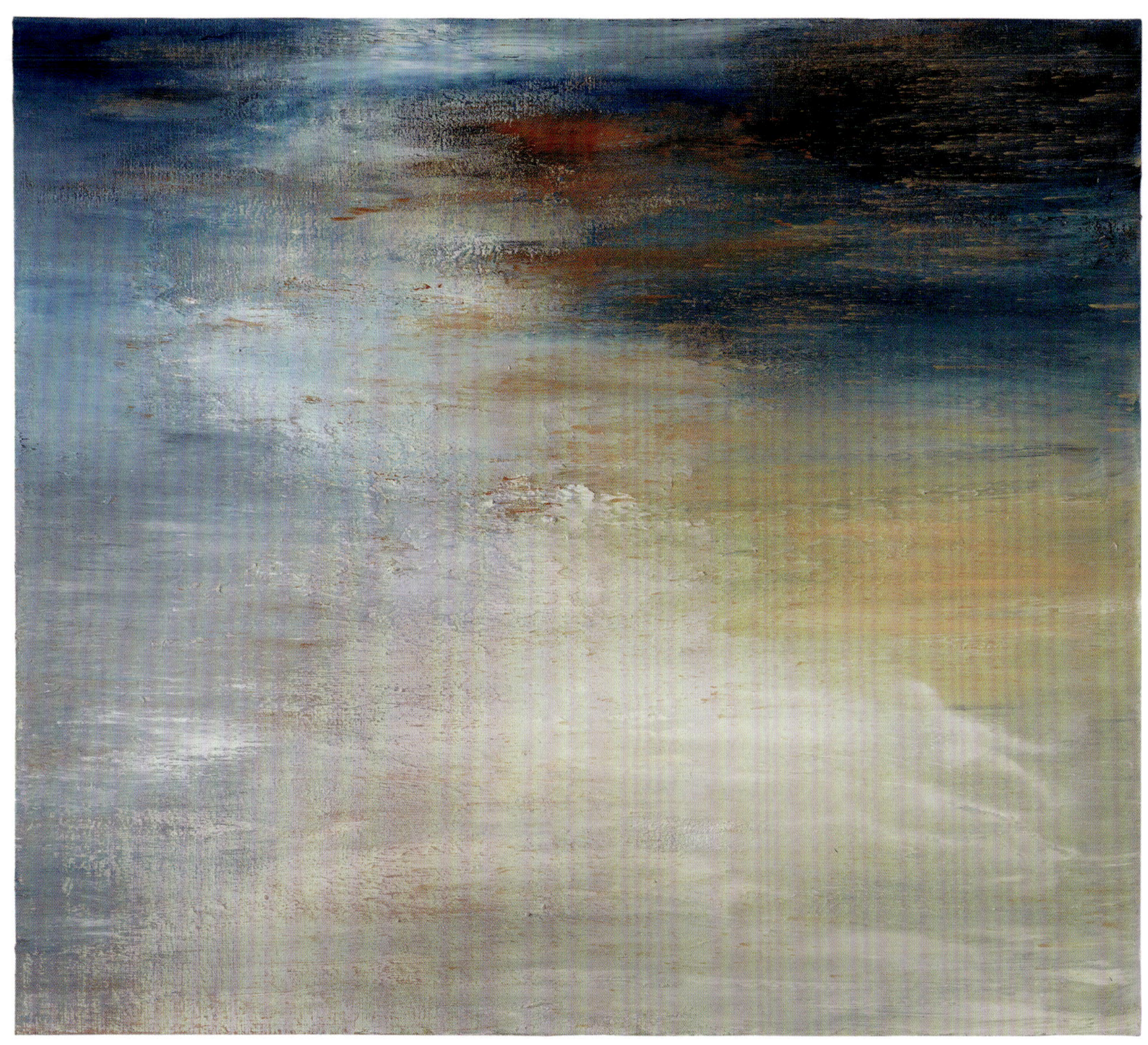

Lunar Diffractions 月亮衍射

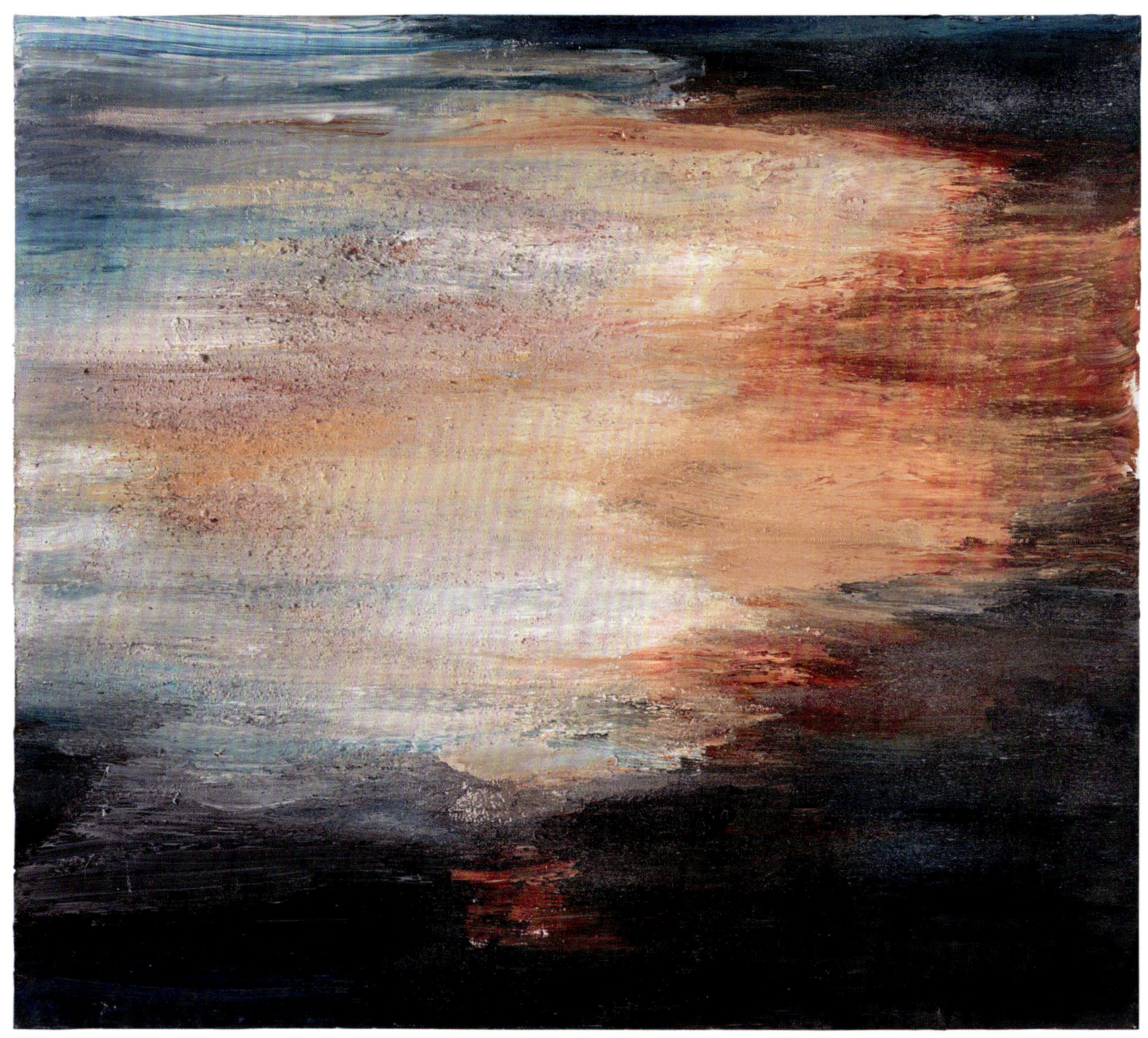

Amplified Visions of the Sky 天空的擴大視像

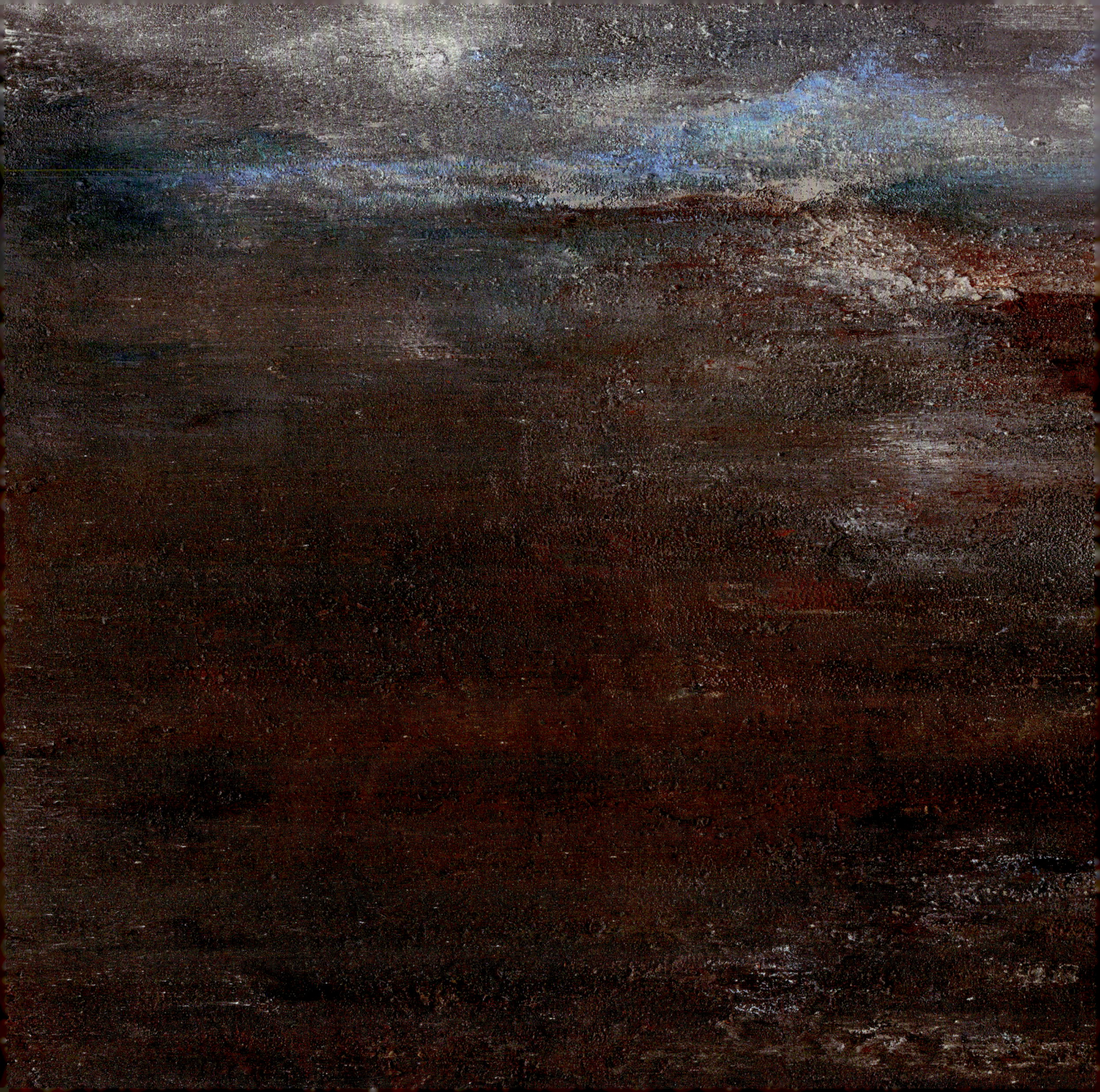

Lunar Reflections 月亮反射

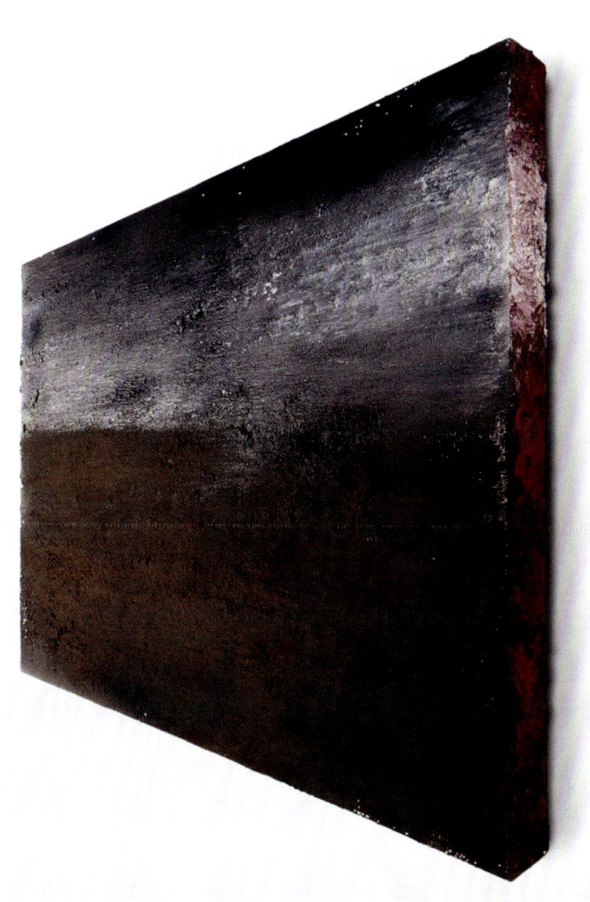

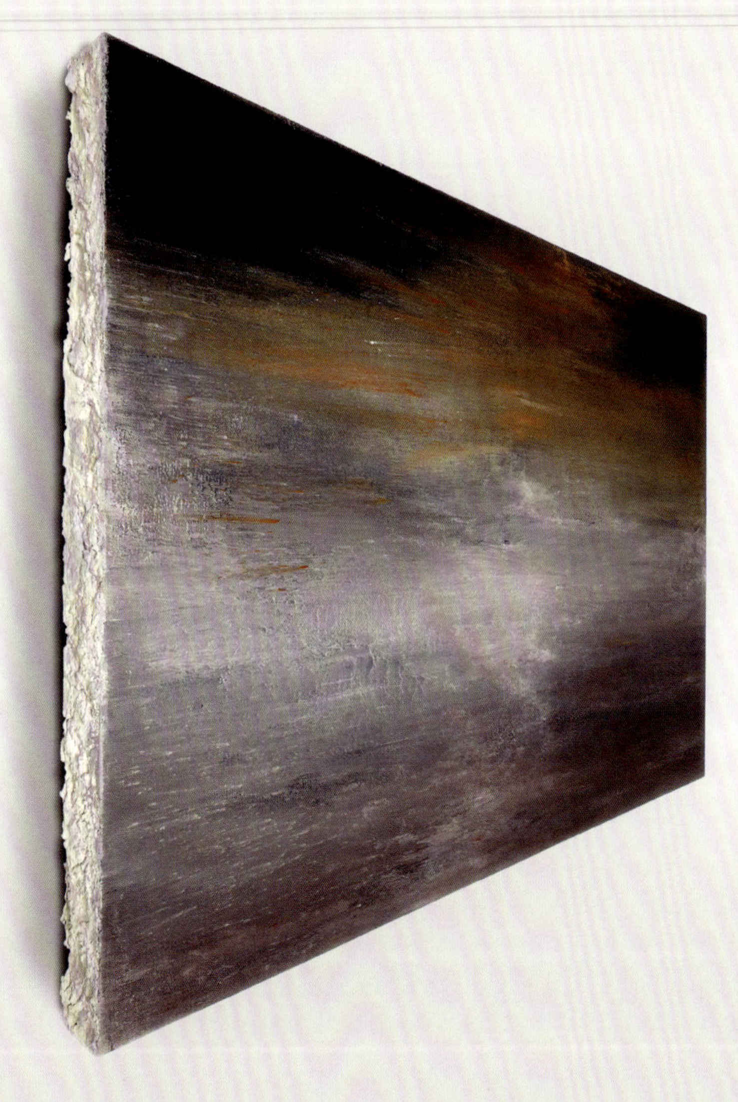

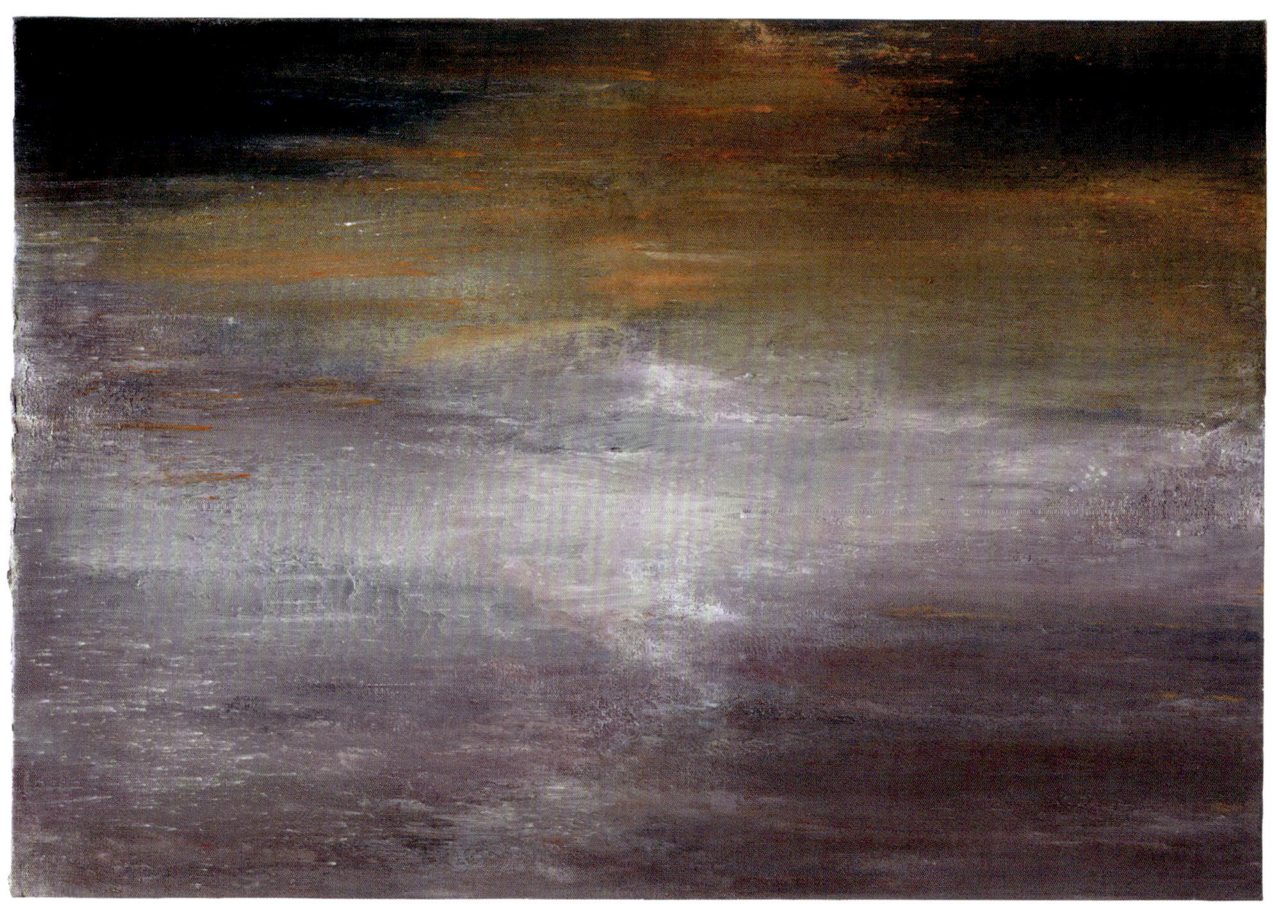

Sides of the Sky 天空的邊

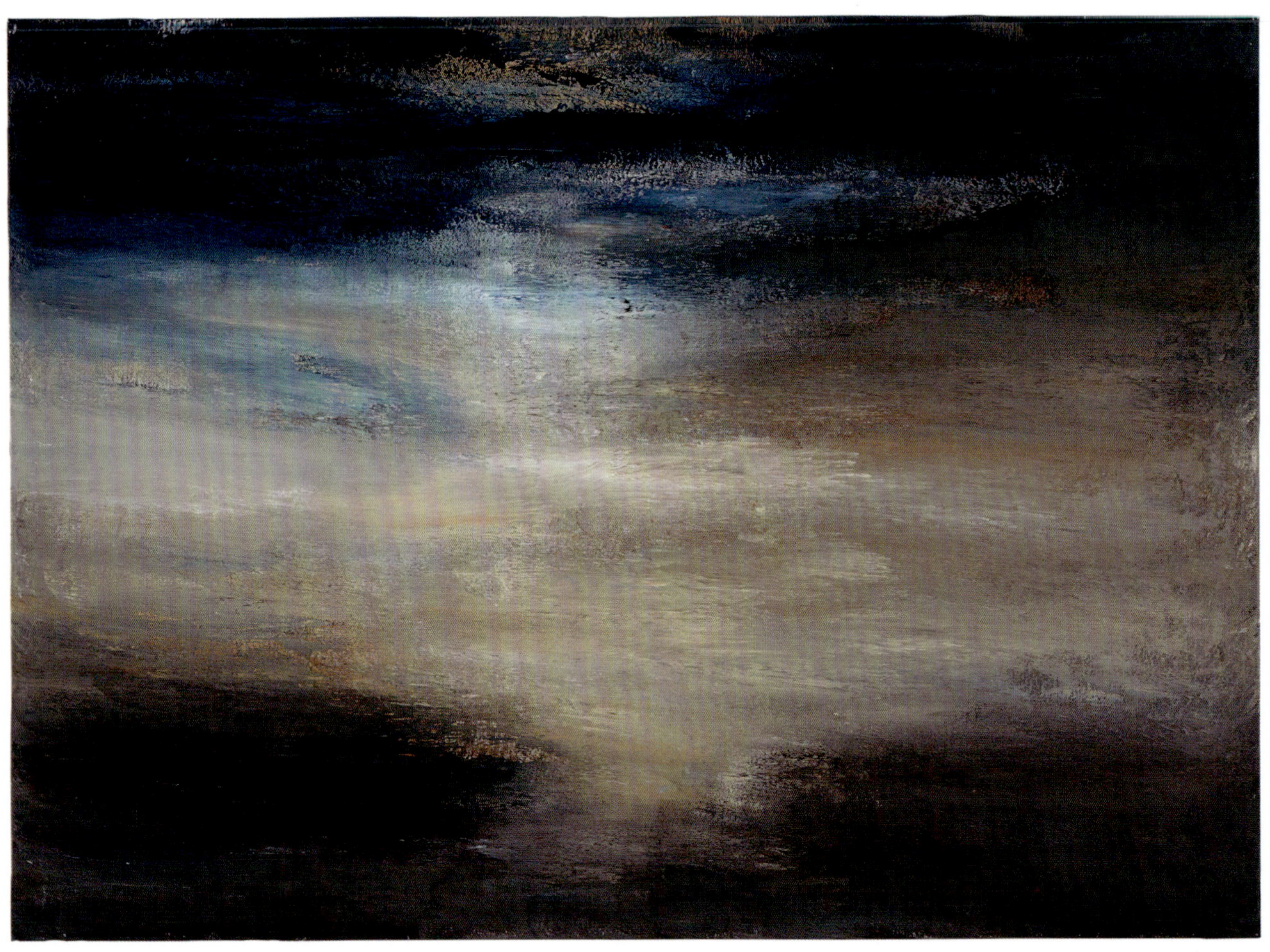

Luminous Horizons 燦爛地平線

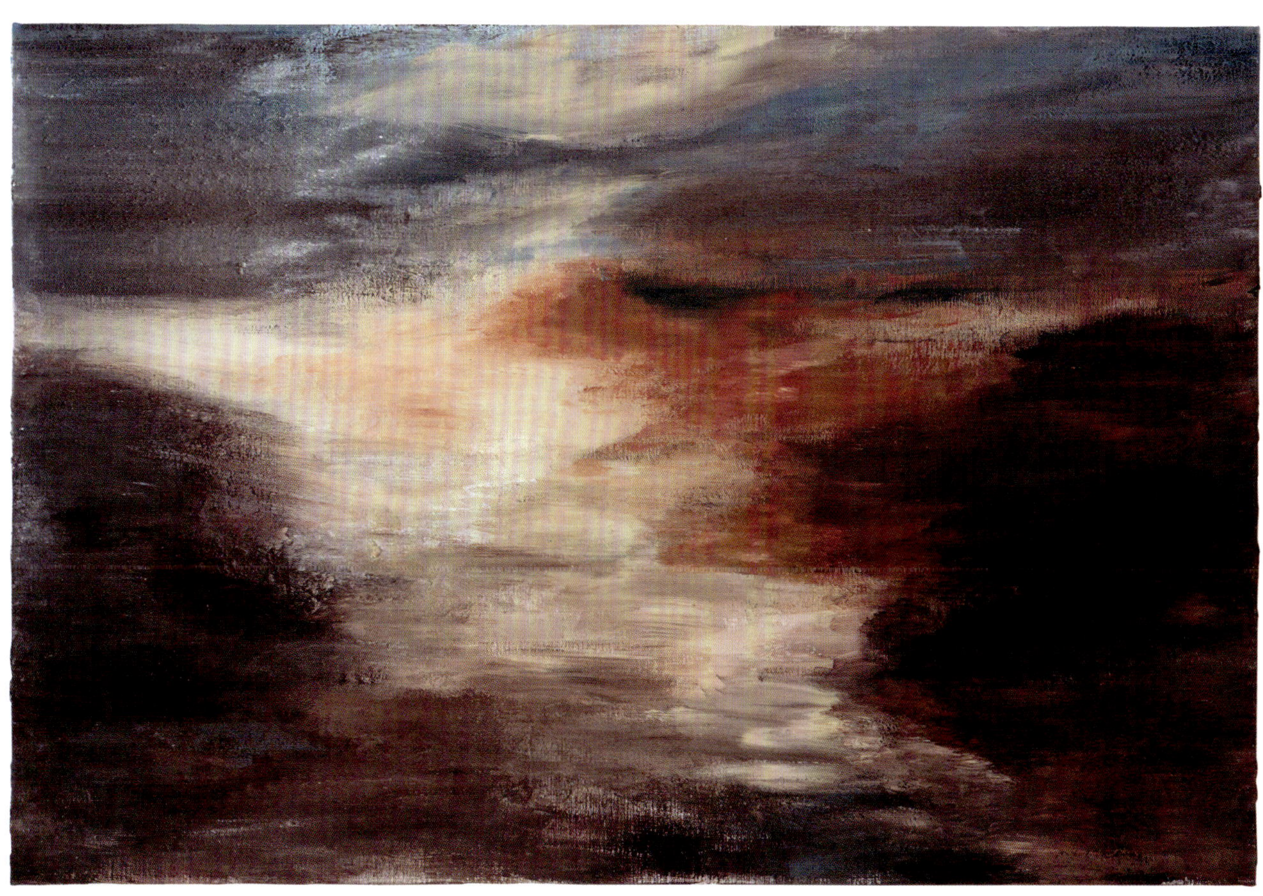

Flashes in Shadow 陰影裏的閃光

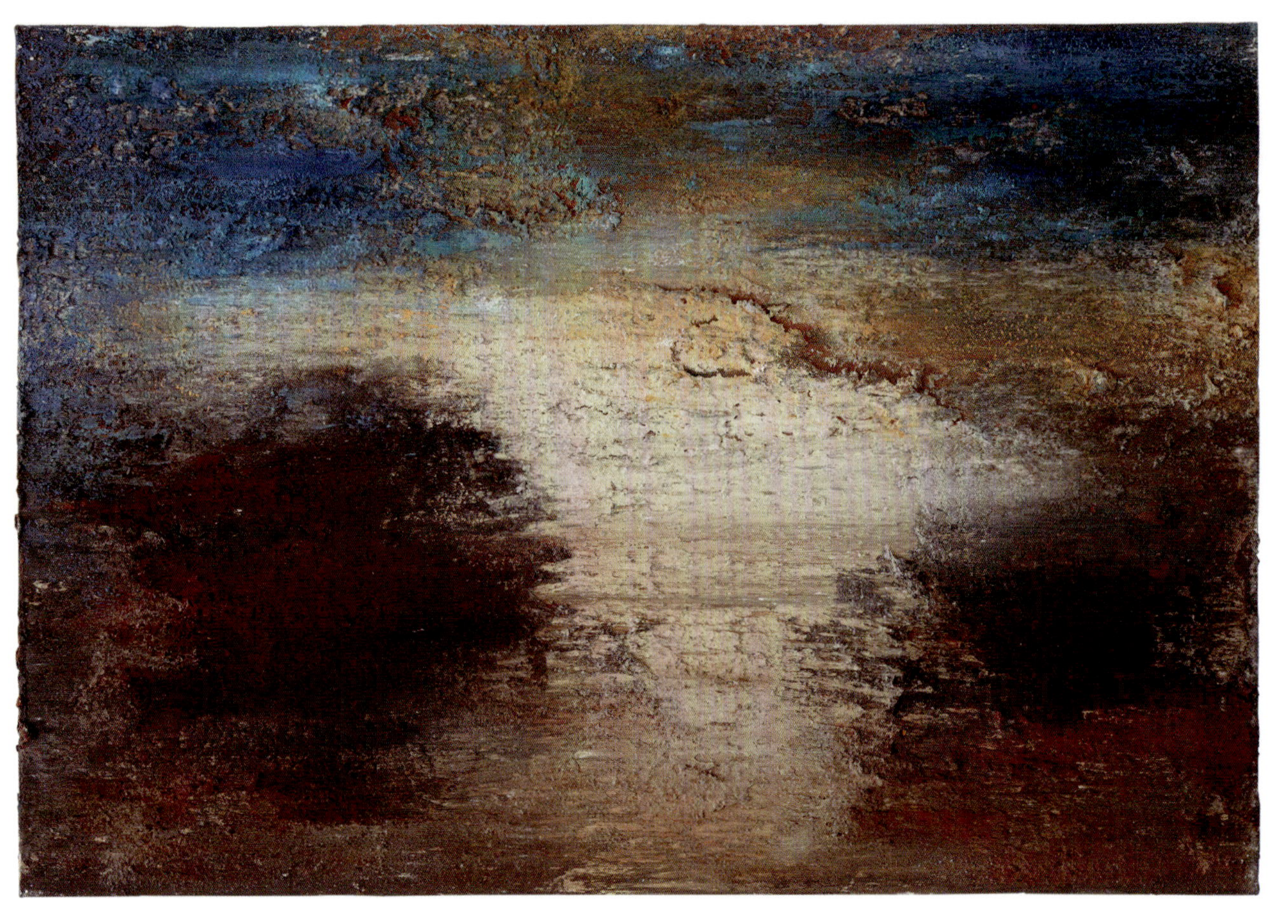

Floating Mountains 浮山

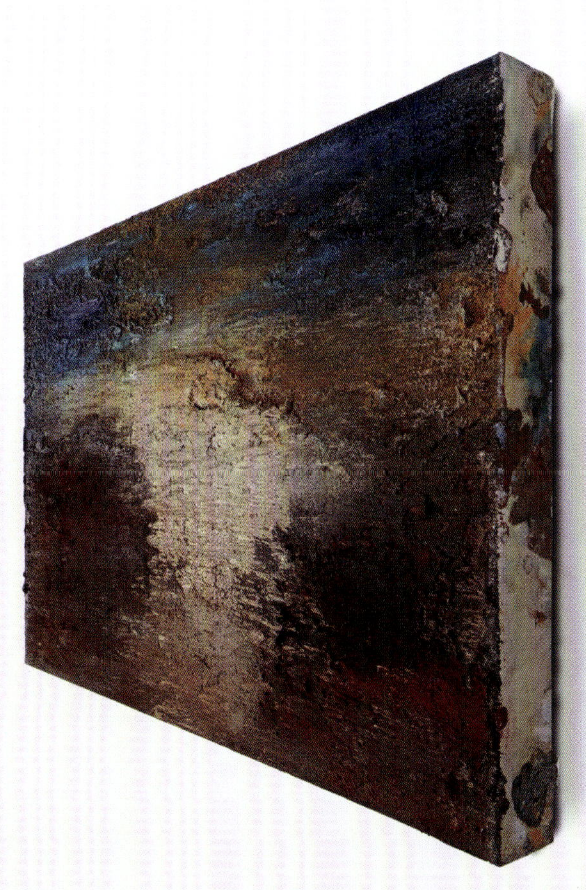

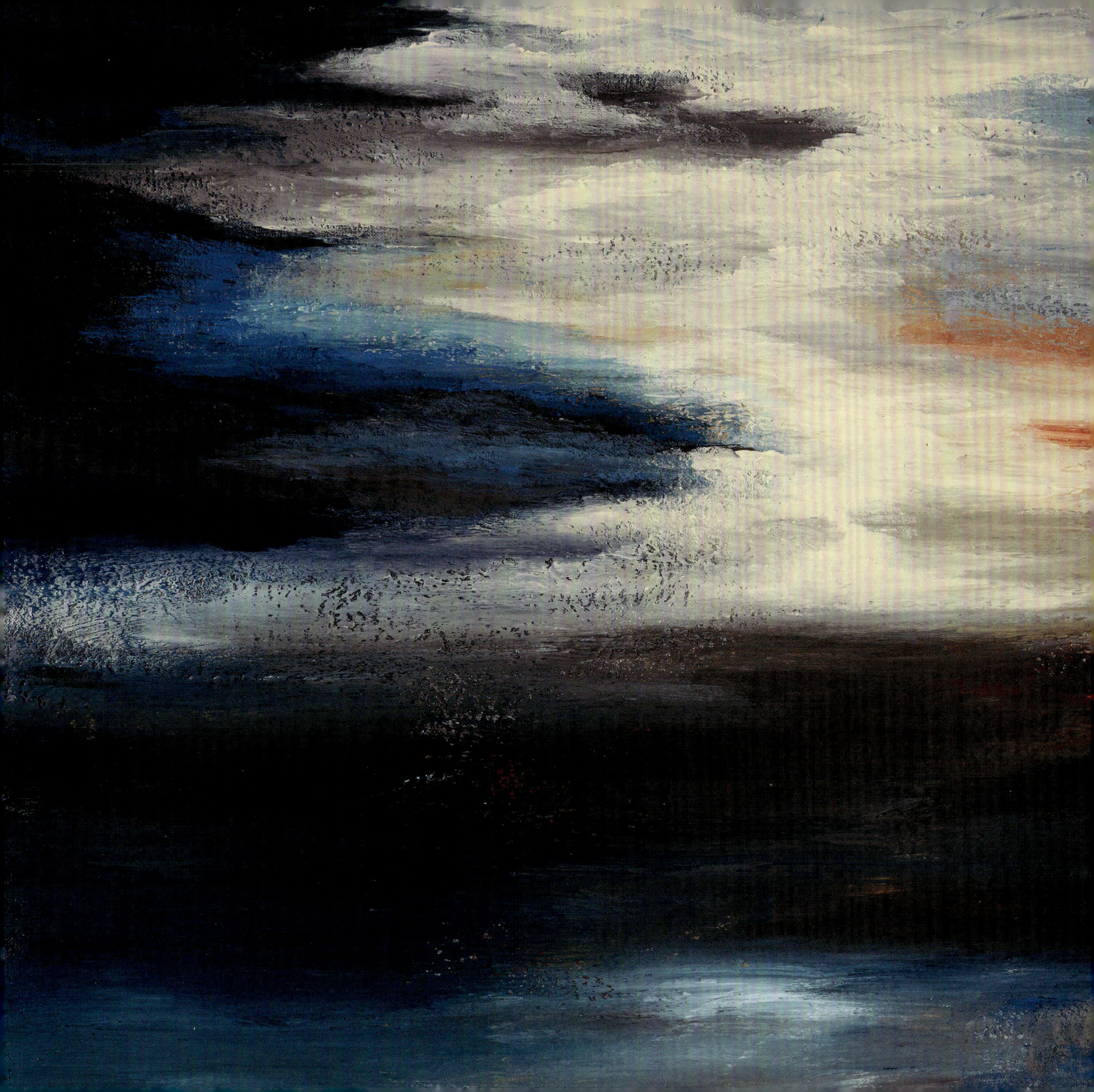

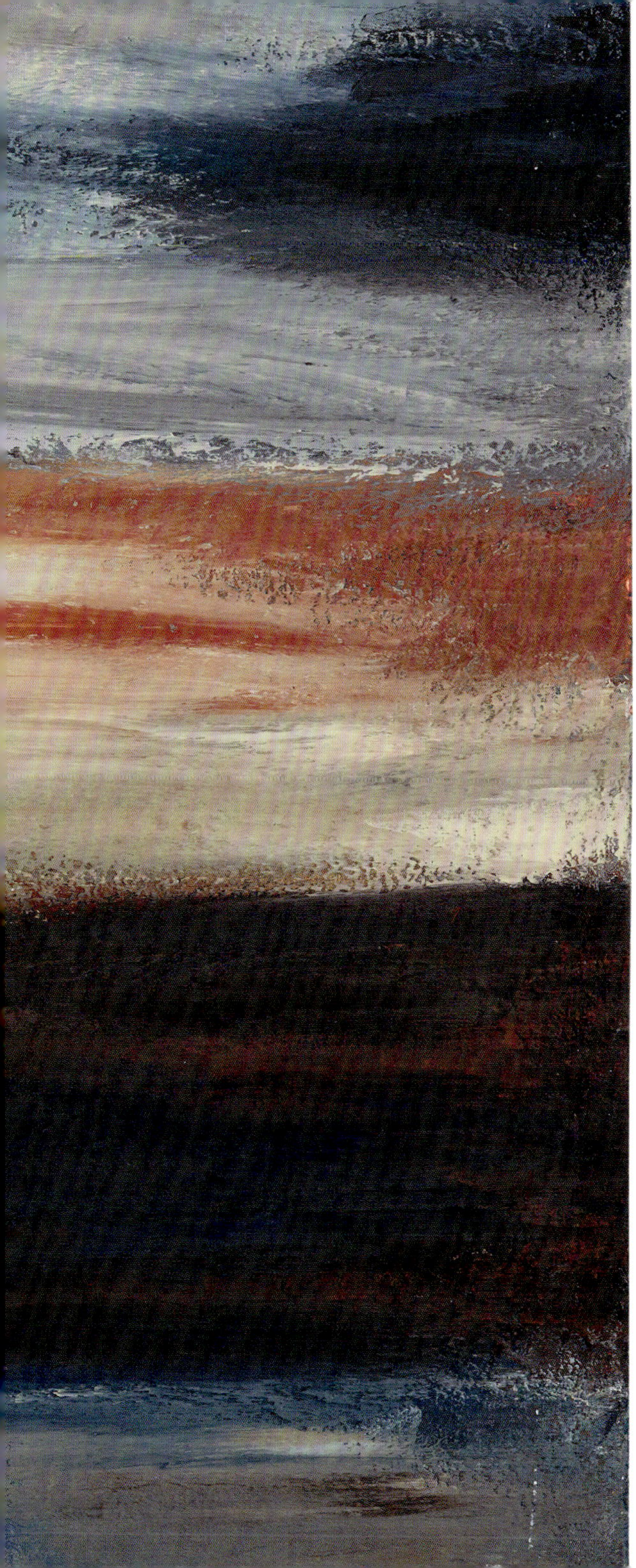

Expansive Evening Lights 擴大暮色

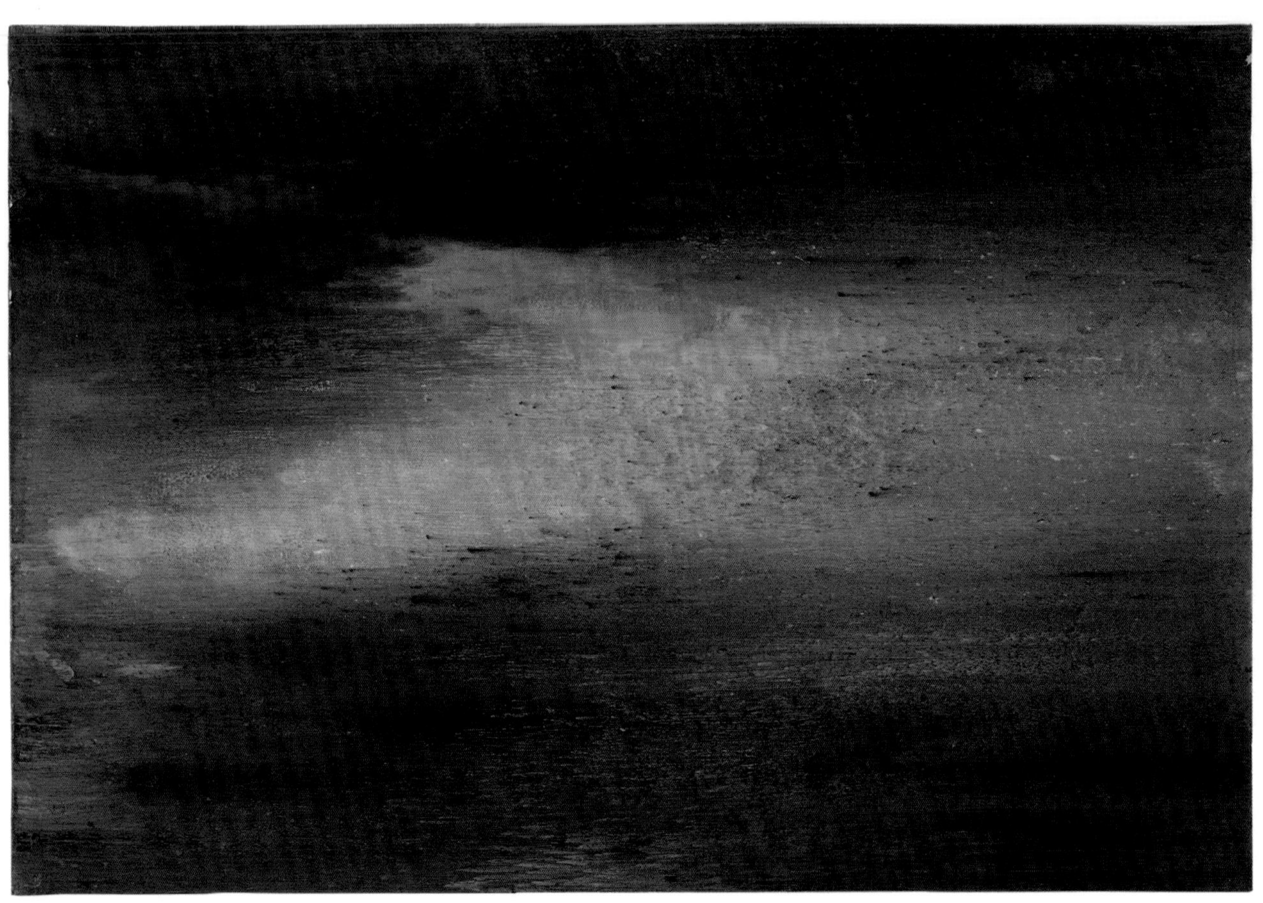

Twilight Mirror 曙光鏡子

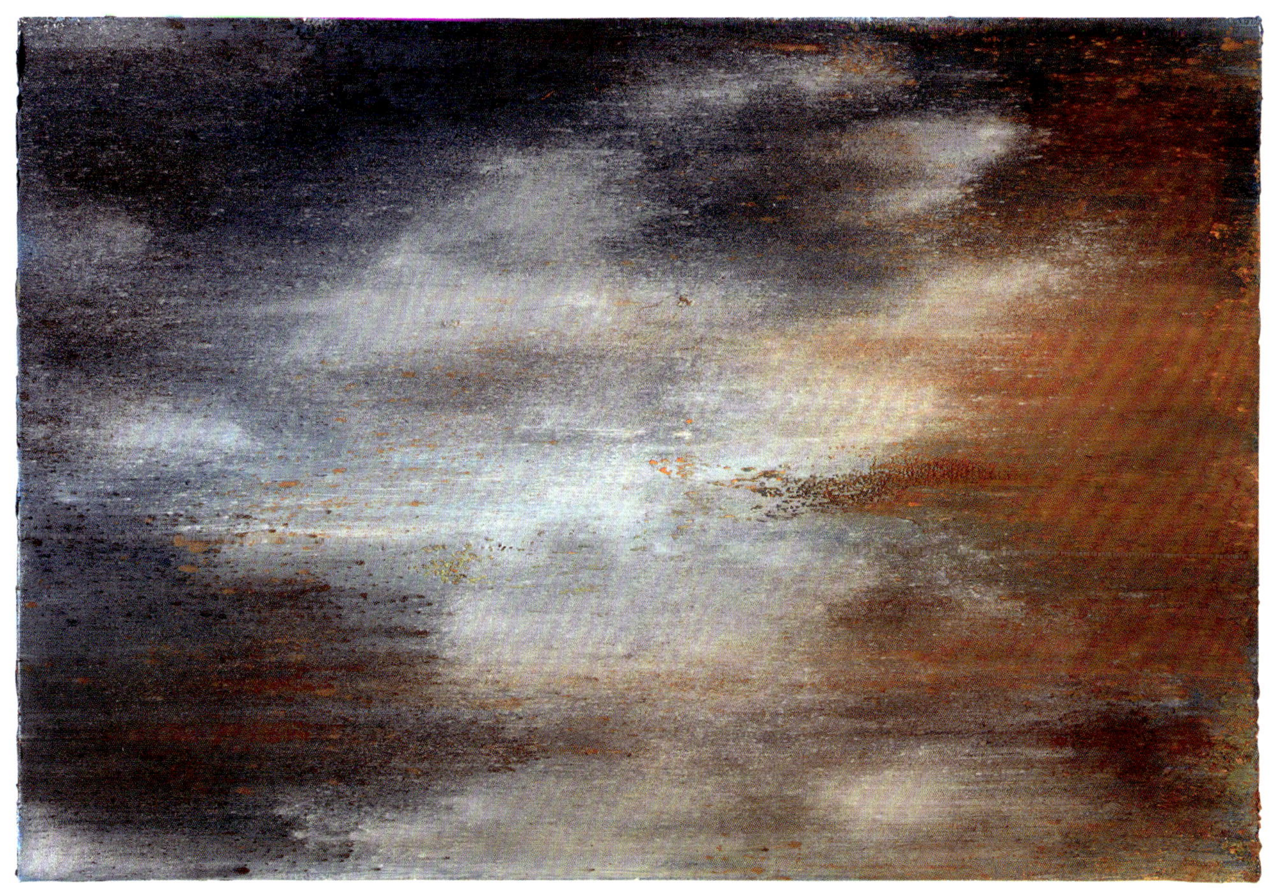

Silver Mists 銀霧

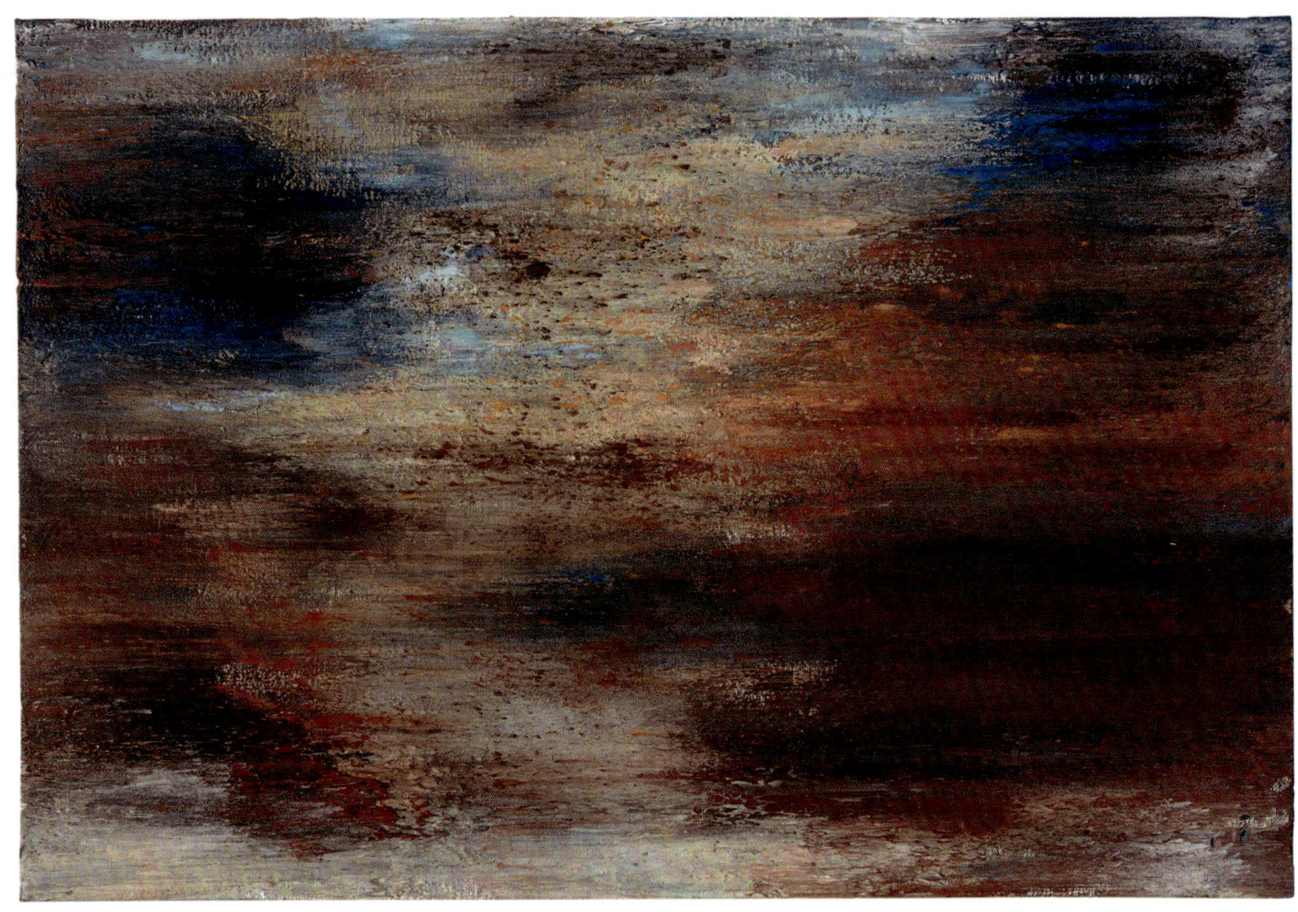

Pigments Glimpsing Night 瞥見顏料之夜

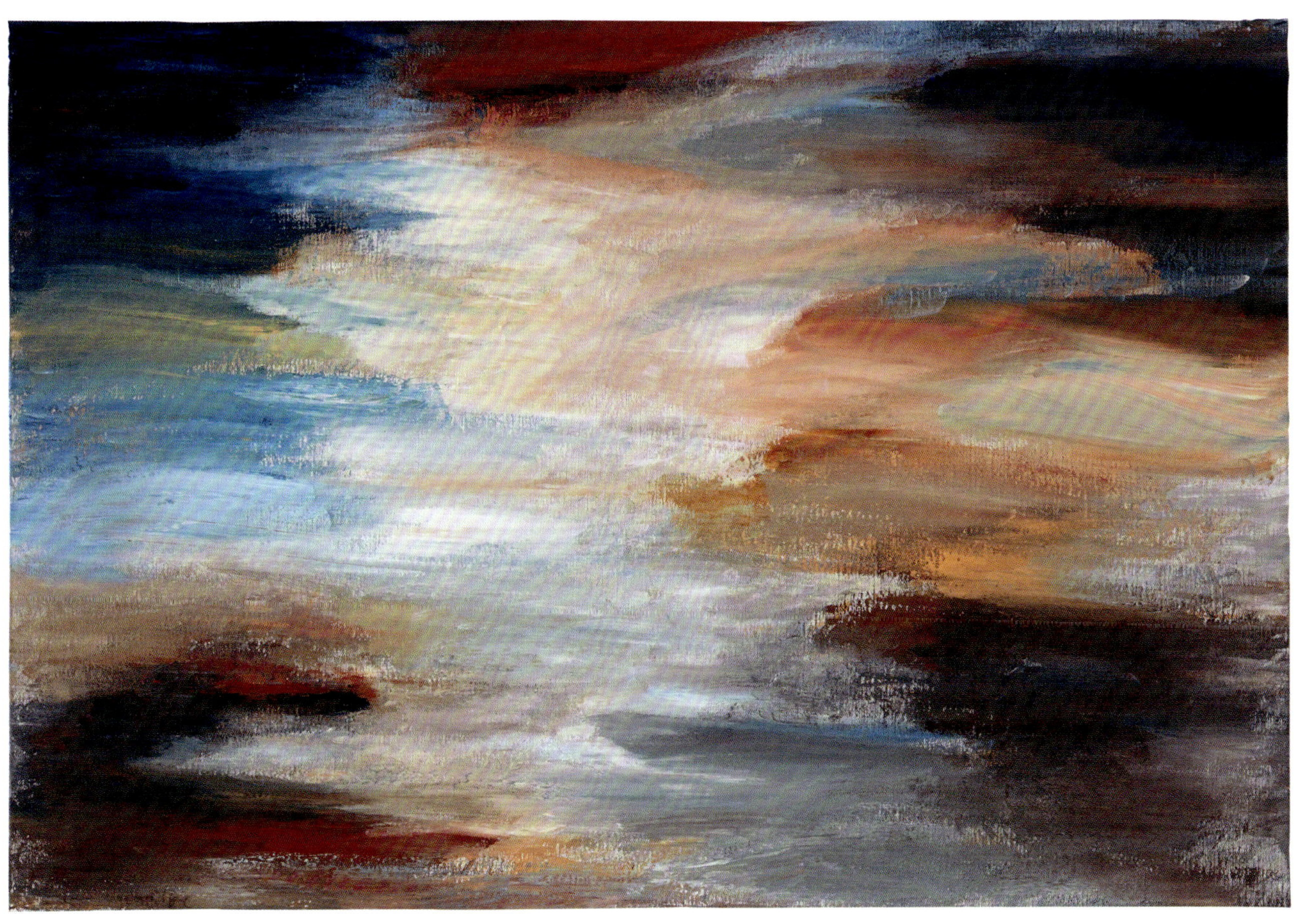

Celestial Brushstrokes 天空筆觸

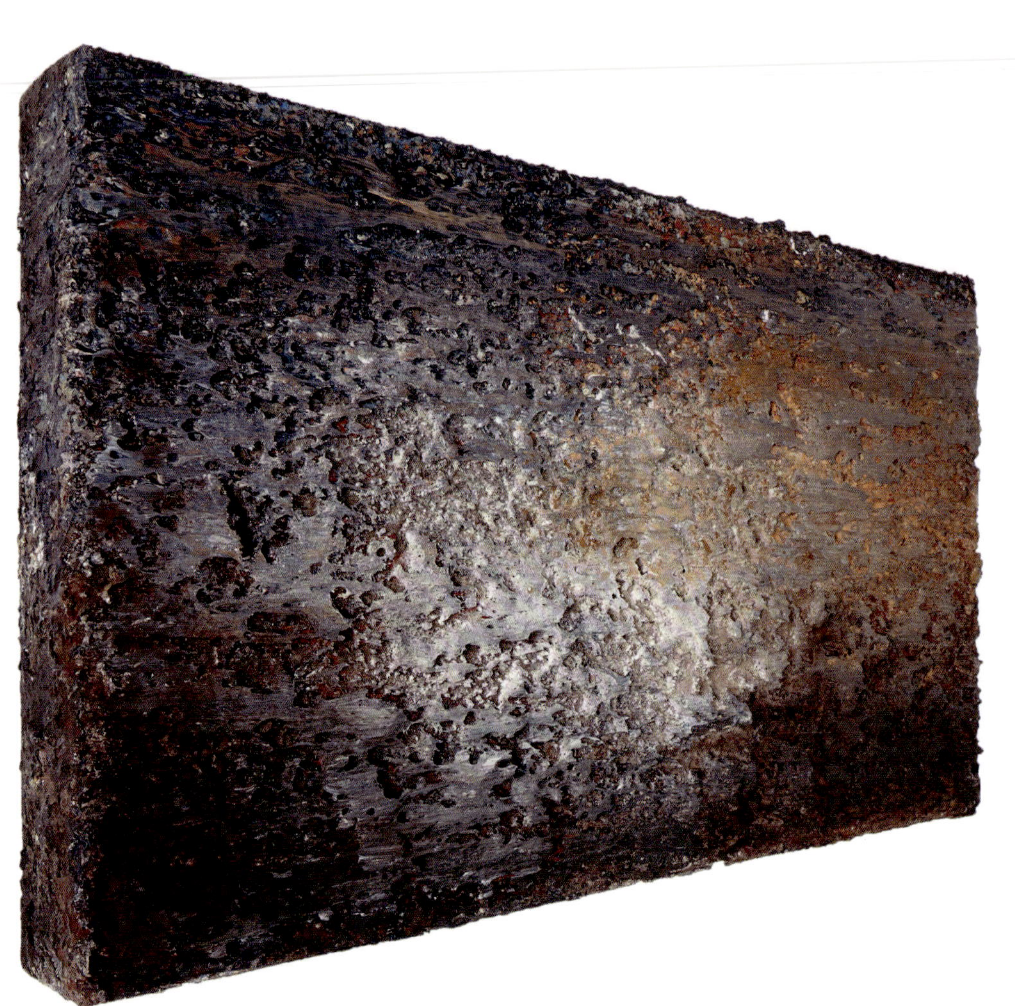

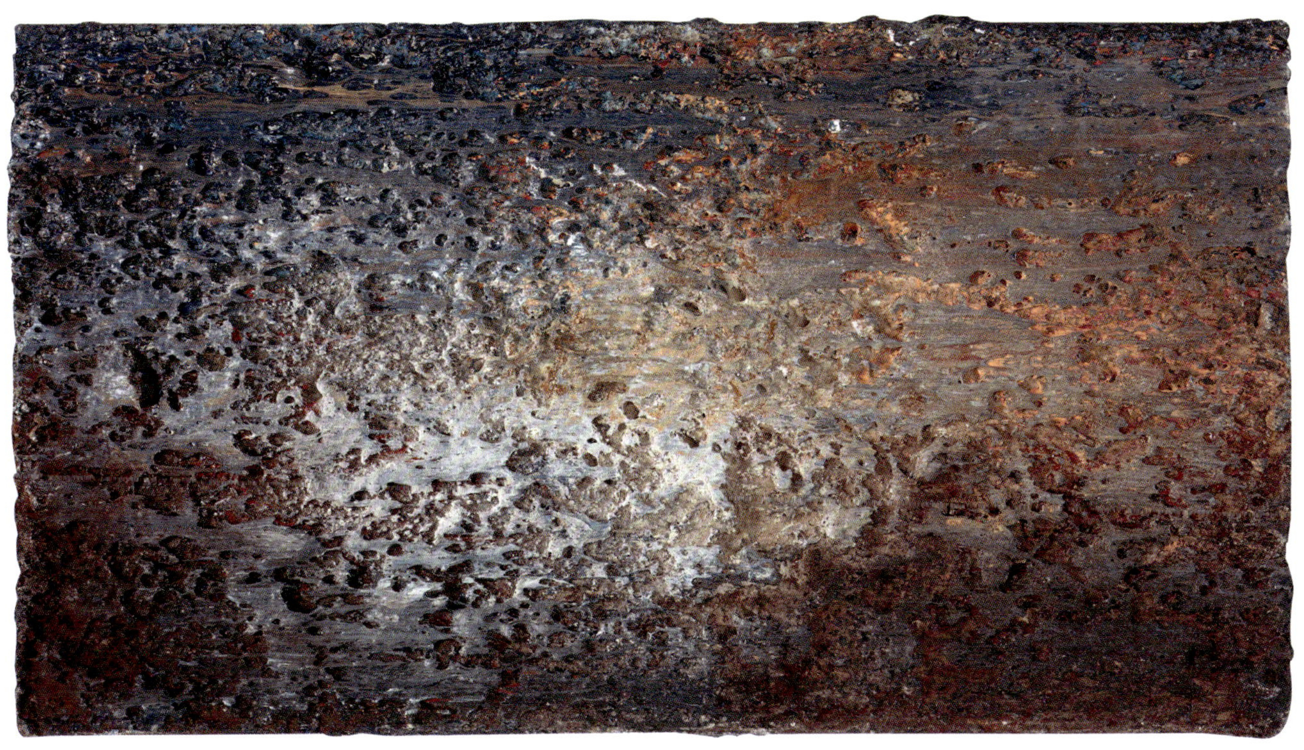

Crust of the Landscape 地形表殼

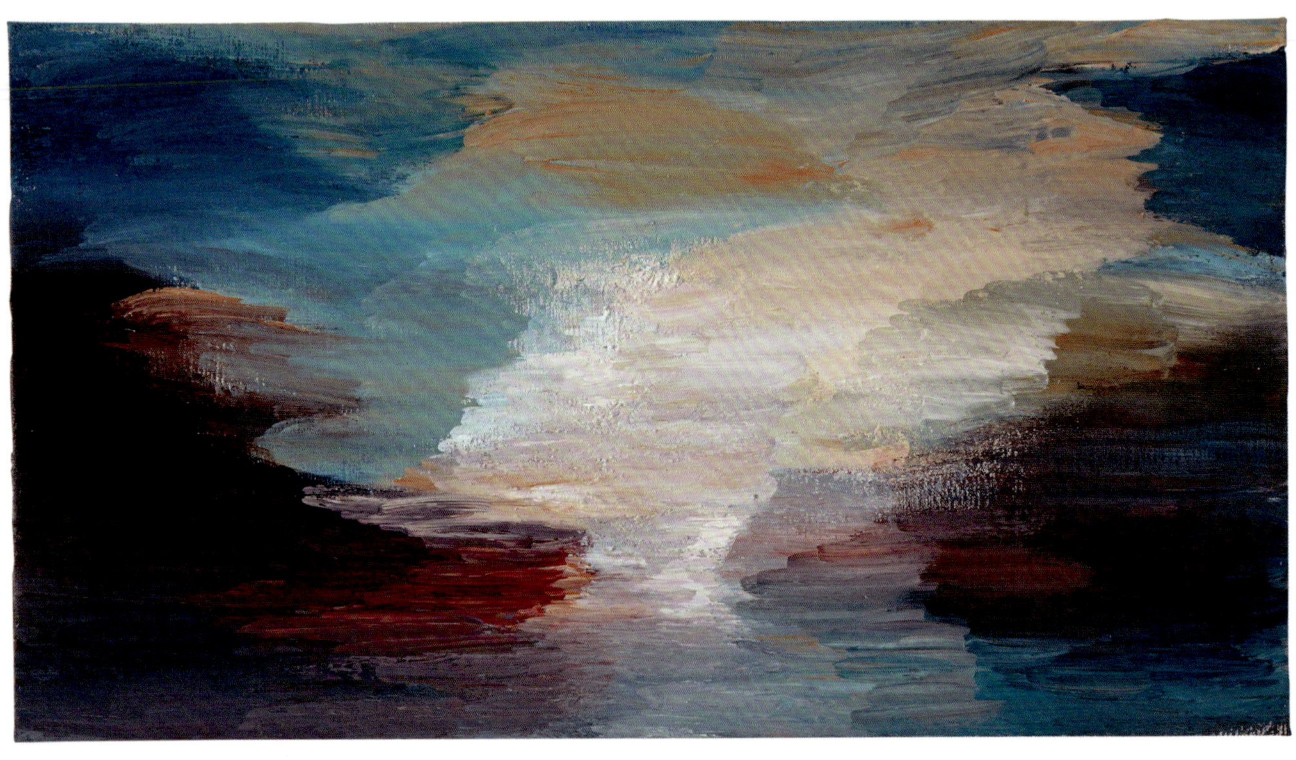

Chromatic Fantasies (Thinking of Jan Pieterszoon Sweelinck) 音階顏色狂想曲（想起揚・彼德松・思維林克）

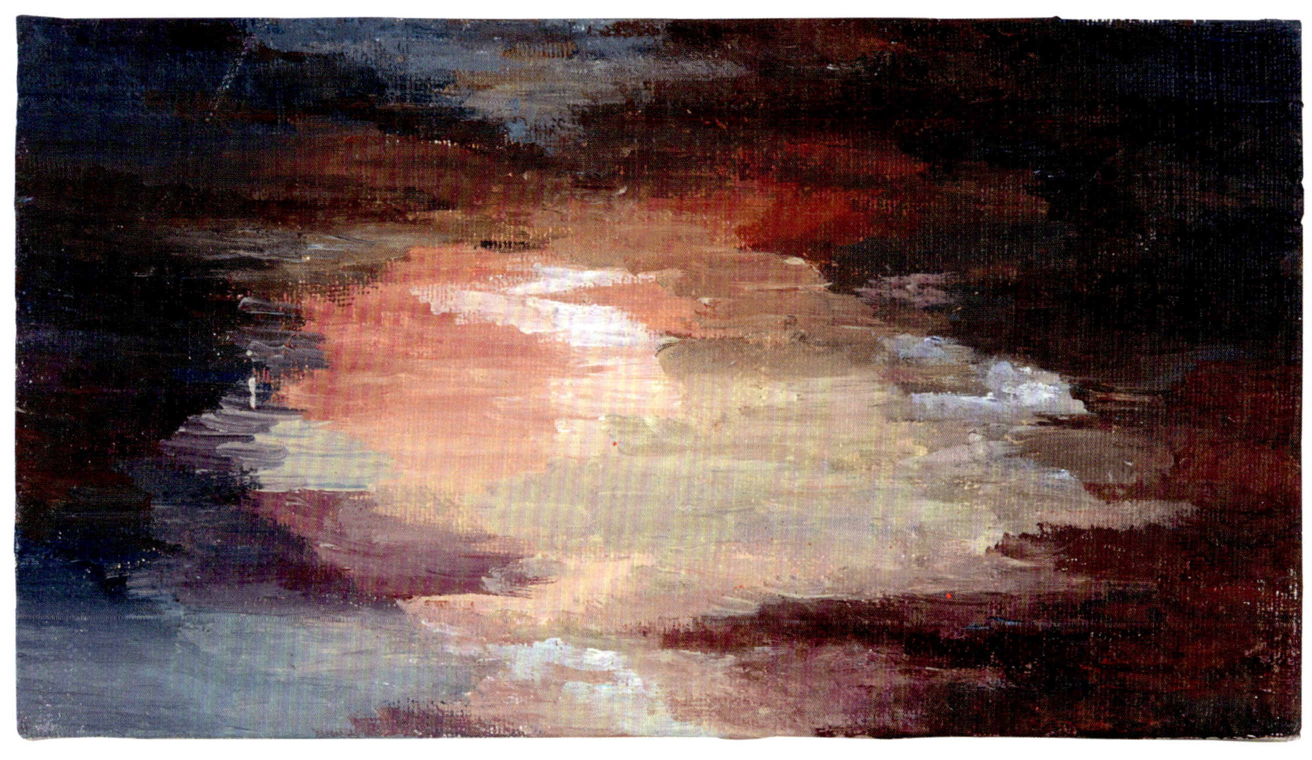

Little Chromatic Fantasies I (Thinking of Jan Pieterszoon Sweelinck) 音階顏色小狂想曲之一（想起揚・彼德松・思維林克）

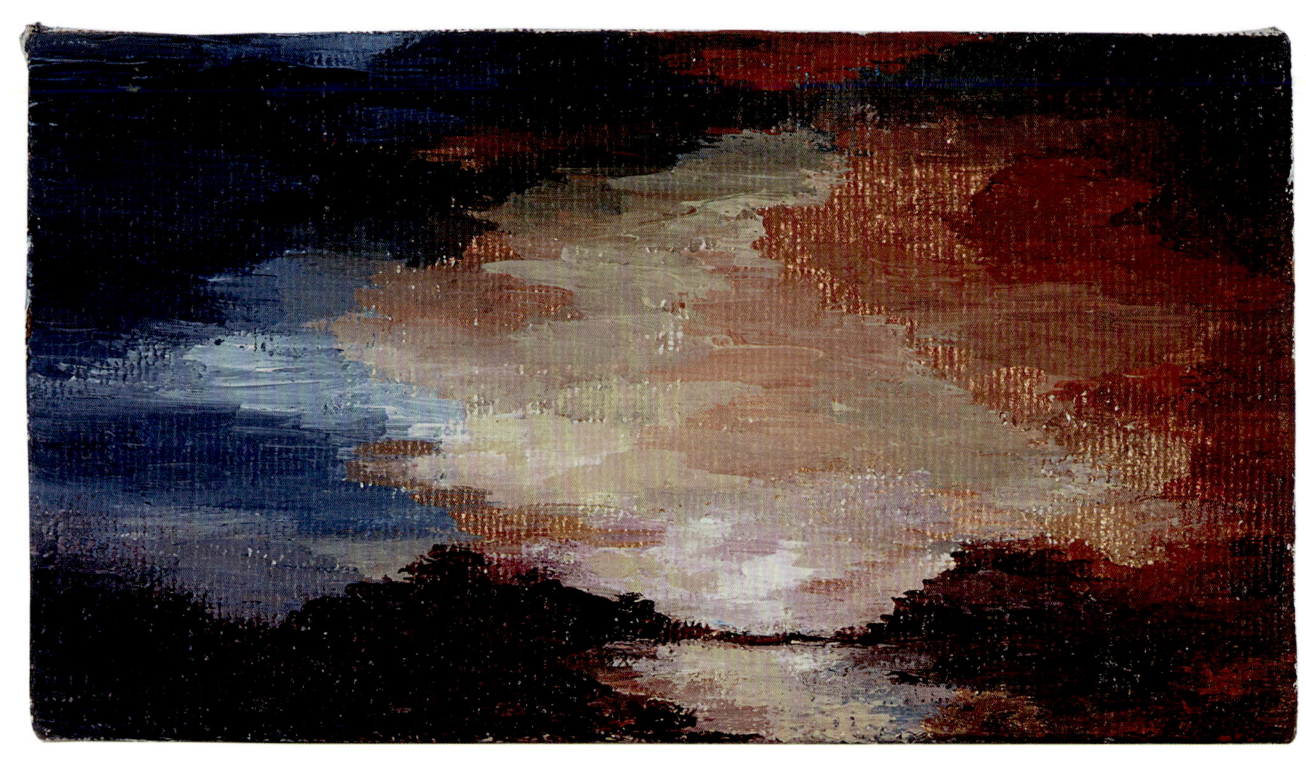

Little Chromatic Fantasies II (Thinking of Jan Pieterszoon Sweelinck) 音階顏色小狂想曲之二（想起揚・彼德松・思維林克）

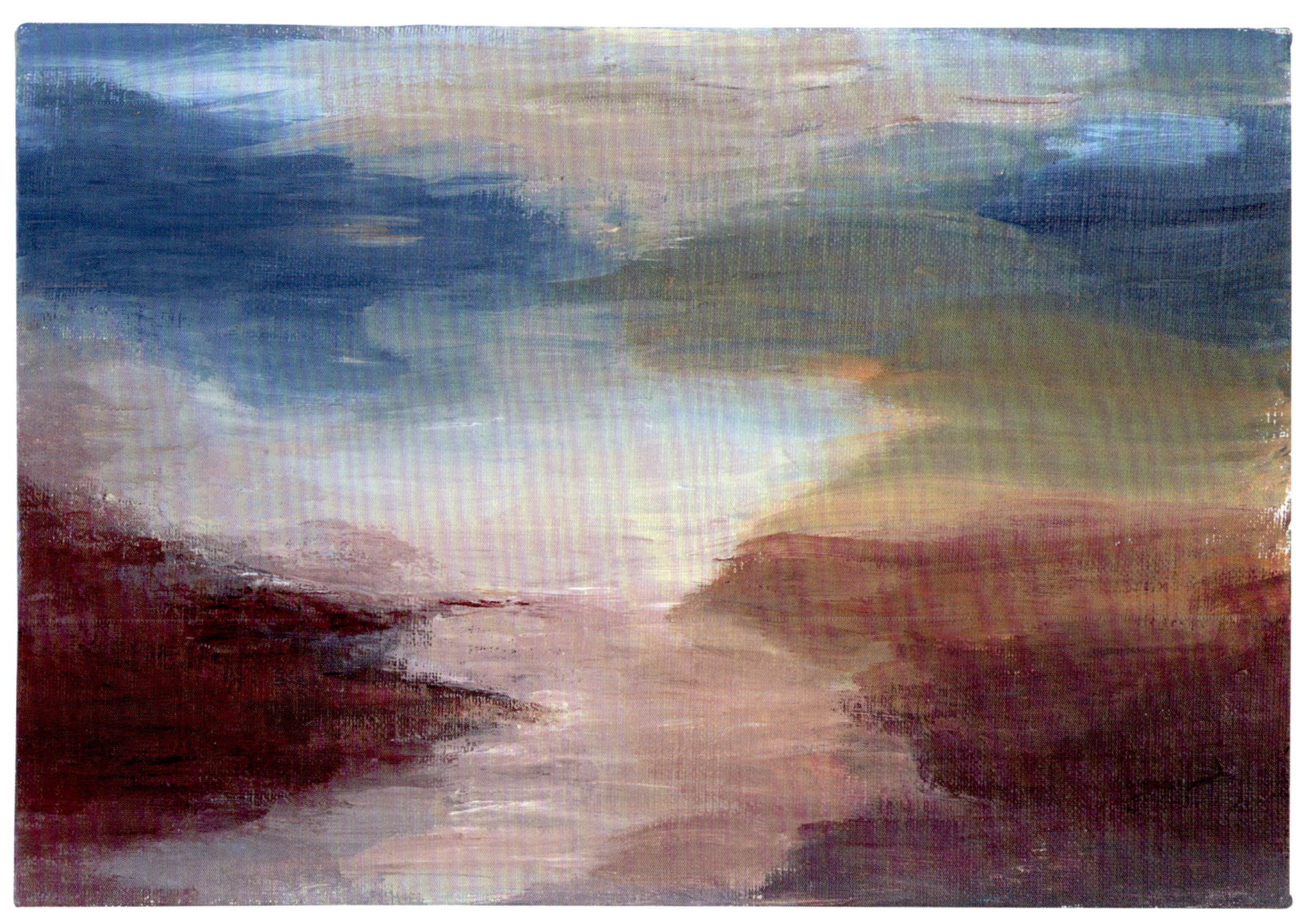

Merging Music and Landscape (Thinking of Unico Wilhelm van Wassenaer) 音樂與風景結合（想起尤奈高．威林．瓦瑟納爾）

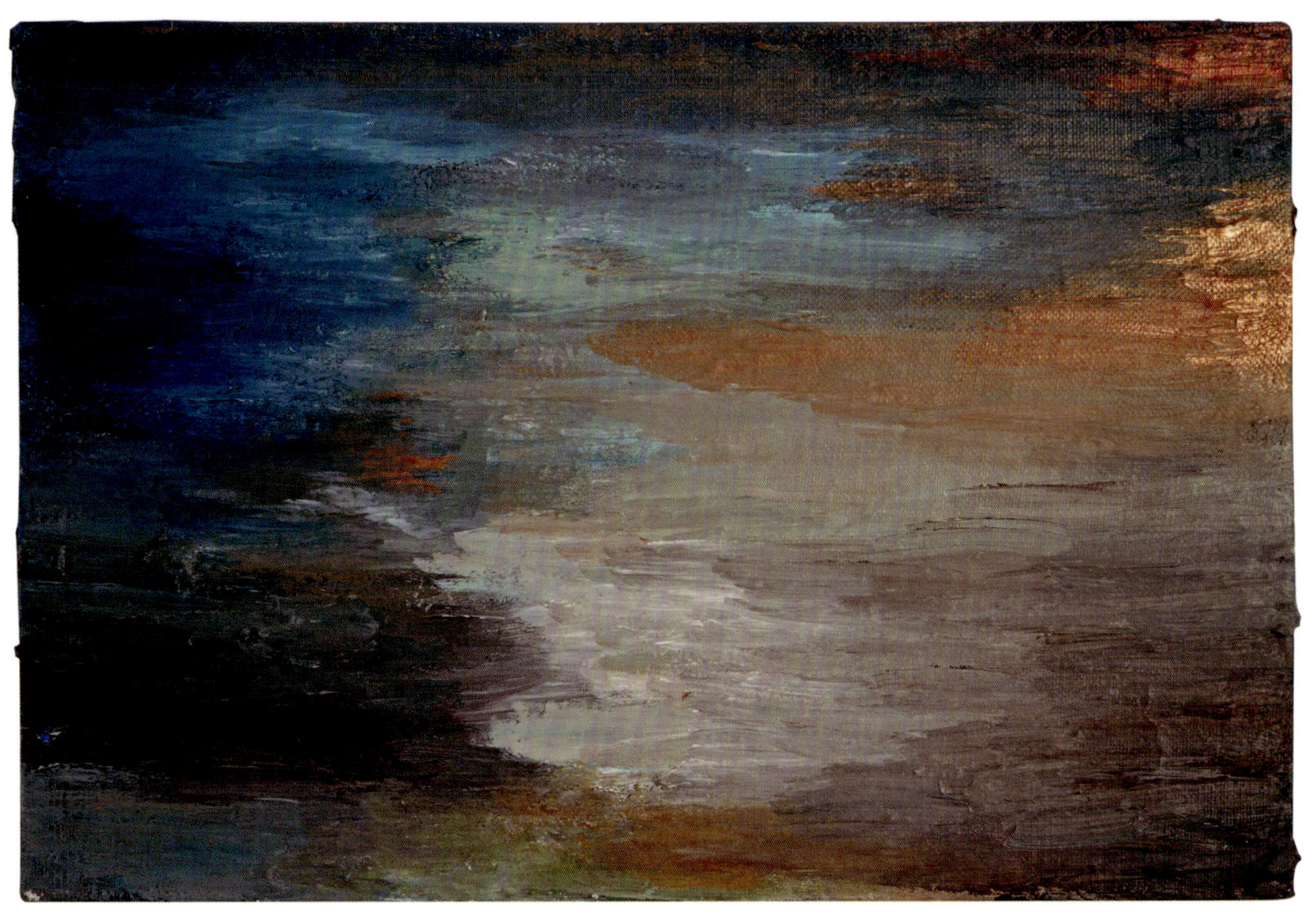

Light Mist 光霧

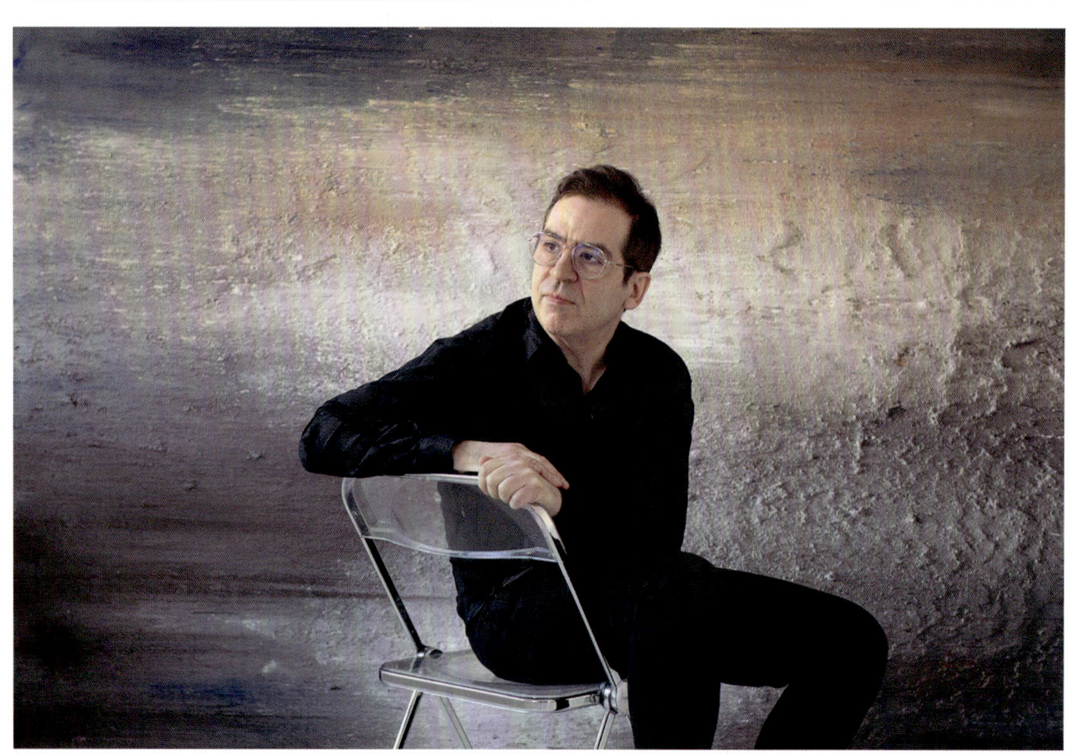

Alberto Reguera 艾拔圖・雷古拉

Biography

Alberto Reguera (Segovia, 1961) is a Spanish artist currently based in Madrid for whom travelling—across Spain and abroad—has become a way of life. For more than three decades, he has developed exhibitions which, through the medium of painting, explore the relationship between space, diverse subject matters and layers of visual depth.

A graduate in Modern History from the University of Valladolid, he moved to Paris to attend the contemporary art seminar L'Art du XXème siècle (École du Louvre). He also took part in the Actual Art Workshops at the Círculo de Bellas Artes in Madrid, with contemporary masters such as Lucio Muñoz. Similarly, he was influenced by another of the most iconic of Spanish artists, Rafael Canogar, who selected Reguera to participate in a joint exhibition at the Museo de Bellas Artes in Seville, Spain, as part of the Relevos project (2002).

As he has woven together exhibitions and extended stays in Madrid and Paris, Reguera has held three solo exhibitions in Washington D.C., culminating in his participation as the only Spanish artist selected for Exhibit E in 2003.

When he first began to show his paintings in Asia in 2007, he had already started to build up the layers of volume, which by then were moving towards the medium of sculpture. A clear indication of this is the Sculpture Square of Singapore staging his project *Beyond Form*, which he subsequently presented at the City Hall of Hong Kong in 2010. In 2012, he moved beyond the limits of the canvas when he created, during a stay in Shanghai, two large expansive paintings for the CEIBS organisation for display in a building designed by I.M. Pei, where he then became artist in residence.

簡歷

艾拔圖．雷古拉，西班牙藝術家，1961年出生於塞哥維亞，現居馬德里。對於藝術家本人來說，旅遊已是一種生活方式。他遊遍西班牙和世界各地，在過去三十多年來舉行的展覽以繪畫為媒介，探索空間、相異題材和視覺深度層次之間的關係。

他畢業於西班牙巴利亞多利德大學，主修近代歷史，畢業後參加巴黎羅浮宮學院舉辦的「二十世紀藝術」當代藝術課程，與盧斯奧．莫尼奧等當代繪畫大師參與馬德里「美術圈」舉辦的「真實藝術工作坊」。與此同時，他也受到另一位著名西班牙藝術大師里法奧．卡諾家的影響，並被卡諾家選入參與西班牙塞維利亞美術博物館的聯合展覽，作為2002年「接力」計劃的一部分。

雷古拉除了在馬德里和巴黎長期居住和舉行展覽之外，也曾在美國首都華盛頓舉行過三場個展，2003年成為唯一獲邀參加該地舉辦的「展品E」的西班牙藝術家。

在2007年首次在亞洲展出作品前，雷古拉已開始在畫布上厚塗顏料，加大畫作的體積，可見他逐漸趨向雕塑創作的領域。在新加坡雕塑廣場舉行「形式之外」的項目後，再於2010年在香港大會堂舉辦展出作品。在2012年停留上海期間，為當地的中歐國際商學院創作兩件巨幅延展畫，突破畫布的空間限制。畫作完成後展陳於由貝聿銘設計的大樓，後來成為該處的駐場藝術家。

In that same year, Reguera showed one of his installation paintings in the Place du Louvre, under the auspices of UNESCO and the Mairie du 1er as part of the Diversité Culturelle International Festival. In 2008, he took part in Assises, another official exhibition in the French capital, at the central office of the Ministère de la Culture et de la Communication and later, in 2013, at the Paris Espace Eiffel 1 de L'École Supérieure du Commerce Extérieur. His exhibitions have extended to other French speaking capitals such as Brussels, where he exhibits regularly, as well as galleries in London, Paris, Madrid, Lisbon and Hong Kong.

Reguera also documents his myriad travels through photography; featured prominently among these series are images from his trips to Norway (1998), Australia and New Zealand (2006 and 2007), with the latter becoming the basis for a solo exhibition at the Paris Cervantes Institute entitled Antipodas.

In 2015, the University Museum and Art Gallery (UMAG), The University of Hong Kong, in collaboration with the Consulate General of Spain in Hong Kong, organised an exhibition with a selection of Reguera's artworks that were made from 2001 to 2015, entitled *Blue Expansive Landscape*.

Reguera also participated in the exhibition *Arte contemporáneo en Palacio. Pintura y escultura en las Colecciones Reales*, organised by Spain's National Heritage, shown at the Royal Palace of Madrid in 2015–16.

In 2016, the Esteban Vicente Museum of Segovia organised his first retrospective exhibition in Spain—*Alberto Reguera: El Aura de la Pintura 1990–2015*.

In 2018, Reguera had his fifth solo show in Hong Kong, where he presented the pictorial performance *Peaceful Mountain* at the Karin Weber Gallery. In 2019 he exhibited at the XX/20 collective in Hong Kong.

同年，雷古拉在羅浮宮廣場展出一幅圖像裝置，作為聯合國教科文組織及第一區市政廳聯合舉辦的國際多元文化節的一部分。2008年，他參加巴黎的另一個官方展覽「Assises」，在法國文化及通訊部中央辦公大樓展出作品，以及2013年在對外貿易高等學院巴黎艾菲爾一號校區舉辦展覽。他的足跡還遍佈布魯塞爾等法語區的國家首都，並在該地定期舉辦展覽，亦在倫敦、巴黎、馬德里、里斯本、香港等城市的畫廊參展。

雷古拉通過攝影紀錄多段旅程。他所拍攝的照片尤以挪威(1998年)、澳洲和紐西蘭(2006年和2007年)的景色最為出衆。後來更以紐西蘭的照片作出發點，演化成日後在巴黎塞萬提斯學院舉辦的個人展覽「對蹠點」。

2015年，香港大學美術博物館與西班牙駐香港總領事館合作，甄選他在2001至2015年間所畫的精品，舉辦名為「悠藍青境」的展覽。

此外，雷古拉還參加過2015至2016年西班牙國家遺產署在馬德里皇宮舉辦的展覽「皇宮裏的當代藝術·皇家藏品中的繪畫與雕塑」。

2016年，位於塞哥維亞的艾斯達班·維森提博物館為他舉辦在西班牙的首個回顧展——「艾拔圖·雷古拉：繪畫的光環1990–2015」。

In 2019 he inaugurated the Hay Festival Segovia 2019 with the pictorial performance *Stelae in Transformation*, the result of which is permanently exhibited at the Municipal Library of Segovia. In this same year he returned to Lisbon and gave a pictorial performance entitled *Shadows of the Wind* at the Instituto Cervantes of Lisbon.

Reguera was selected for the 8th International Biennale of Beijing 2019 at the National Art Museum of China (NAMOC).

In 2020 in Beijing he exhibited the expansive painting he had produced during his live performance at the Delegation of the European Union to China. The artist was inspired by the 38 European Cultural Routes presented to China in the form of an exhibition.

In 2021, he held an exhibition at the Thyssen-Bornemisza, where he also made a pictorial performance. He was selected to participate in Mostra Espanha 2021, Lisbon. This exhibition was organised by the Ministry of Culture and Sports of Spain in collaboration with the Government of Portugal and the Embassy of Spain in Lisbon. Also in 2021, he was the only Spaniard selected to participate in the Cairo International Art District, with the support of the Spanish Embassy in Egypt.

His music collaborations have resulted in two performances—one in 1994 and another in 2001—at the Stedelijk Museum in Amsterdam with the Dutch musician Bart Spaan, who composed and played two musical pieces inspired by his paintings. He also has collaborated with French poets Andrée Chedid and Gilles Mentré, and with Spanish poet Francisco Pino.

Among his most noteworthy prizes are honours from L'Académie des Beaux-Arts of L'Institut de France for the Young Painting competition in 1995 (La Bourse Annuelle de Peinture)

2018年，雷古拉第五次在香港舉辦個展，於凱倫偉伯畫廊進行圖畫表演藝術《和平山》；作品於翌年在香港 XX/20 展出。

2019年，他以另一個圖畫表演藝術《轉型中的碑版》作為塞哥維亞海伊文學藝術節的開幕節目。表演完成後，該作在塞哥維亞市立圖書館永久展出。同年，他前往葡萄牙里斯本，在塞萬提斯學院進行圖畫表演藝術《風的影子》。

雷古拉的作品入選由中國美術館舉行的2019年第八屆中國北京國際美術雙年展。

2020年，他在北京展出早前於歐盟駐華代表團進行現場表演的延展畫。作品的靈感來自該組織在中國舉辦的「三十八條歐洲文化路線」展覽。

2021年，他在馬德里提森．博內米薩博物館舉辦展覽，其中亦進行了圖畫表演藝術。他亦入選了里斯本舉辦的「顯示西班牙2021」。該展覽由西班牙文化體育部、葡萄牙政府和西班牙駐里斯本大使館聯合舉辦。同年，他獲得西班牙駐埃及大使館支持，成為唯一獲選參與開羅國際藝術區項目的西班牙藝術家。

雷古拉與音樂家的合作分別促成於1994年和2001年的兩場表演。兩次演出均在阿姆斯特丹市立博物館舉行。荷蘭音樂家伯德．史班更因受到雷古拉的繪畫所啟發，創作了兩首曲目，並親自演奏。其他與雷古拉合作過

and the Ojo Crítico presented by Radio Nacional de España in 2001.

Reguera's works are included in a number of significant public and private collections, including: the CEIBS Collection, Shanghai; OECD Collection, Paris; Marc Moyens Estate, Washington D.C.; Juan March Foundation Museum, Palma, Spain; Testimoni Collection, La Caixa, Barcelona; Delegation for the European Union to China, Beijing; M.Y. Foundation, Seoul, South Korea; Brigitte and Jacques Gairard Collection, France; Ph Delaunay Collection, Paris; Cynorrhodon-FALDAC, France; Contemporary Art Museum Esteban Vicente, Segovia, Spain; Provincial Council of Palencia, Spain; Museum of Contemporary Art of the City of Madrid; Zurich Financial Services, Switzerland; and the Junta de Castilla y León Collection, Spain. Finally, several of Reguera's works are held in the Royal Collections of Spain's National Heritage.

的，包括法國詩人安德烈．佘蒂和吉勒．蒙特，以及西班牙詩人佛朗西斯高．邊努。

雷古拉曾榮獲多個獎項，包括1995年法蘭西學會美術院青年畫家比賽的年度繪畫獎學金，以及2001年西班牙國立電台頒發的「評論家之眼」獎。

雷古拉的作品被很多重要公營及私營機構收藏，當中包括：中歐國際商學院藏品(上海)、經濟合作暨發展組織收藏(巴黎)、馬可．莫恩斯遺產基金(華盛頓)、琿．馬克基金博物館(西班牙帕爾馬)、德斯達蒙尼收藏(巴塞隆拿凱克薩銀行)、歐盟駐華代表(北京)、M.Y.基金會(南韓首爾)、碧姬及雅克．智夏收藏(法國)、Ph．德努內收藏(巴黎)、Cynorrhodon-FALDAC(法國)、艾斯達班．維森提當代藝術博物館(西班牙塞哥維亞)、帕倫西亞省議會(西班牙)、馬德里市立當代藝術博物館、蘇黎世財務服務組織(瑞士)、卡斯蒂利亞-萊昂議會收藏(西班牙)等。西班牙國家遺產署的皇家珍藏亦藏有數件雷古拉的作品。

List of Paintings 畫目

Moonlit Landscape with a Road beside a Canal
(ca. 1645–50) Aert van der Neer
皓月河旁徑 （約1645–50）阿爾特 · 范 · 德 · 尼爾
35.6 x 65.6 cm / 厘米
Museo Nacional Thyssen-Bornemisza, Madrid, inv. 299 (1931.3)
提森-博內米薩國家博物館， 馬德里，編號: 299 (1931.3)

Illuminated Night 亮夜
2020, Mixed media on canvas 布本混合媒介
220 x 180 x 10 cm / 厘米
Artist's collection 藝術家收藏

Immense Sky, Distant Horizon 曠天遠地
2020, Mixed media on canvas 布本混合媒介
179.9 x 219.9 x 10 cm / 厘米
Artist's collection 藝術家收藏

Lighting Routes 照亮路徑
2020, Mixed media on canvas 布本混合媒介
150 x 220 x 8 cm / 厘米
Artist's collection 藝術家收藏

Night Glare 夜裏光焰
2019, Mixed media on canvas 布本混合媒介
61.6 x 91.5 x 7.5 cm / 厘米
Artist's collection 藝術家收藏

Lunar Diffractions 月亮衍射
2019, Mixed media on canvas 布本混合媒介
132 x 151 x 7.5 cm / 厘米
Artist's collection 藝術家收藏

Amplified Visions of the Sky 天空的擴大視像
2019, Mixed media on canvas 布本混合媒介
132 x 151 x 7.5 cm / 厘米
Artist's collection 藝術家收藏

The Painting Field 繪畫場域
2020, Mixed media on canvas 布本混合媒介
101 x 151 x 7.5 cm / 厘米
Artist's collection 藝術家收藏

Lunar Reflections 月亮反射
2019, Mixed media on canvas 布本混合媒介
101 x 151 x 7.5 cm / 厘米
Artist's collection 藝術家收藏

Sides of the Sky 天空的邊
2019, Mixed media on canvas 布本混合媒介
101 x 151 x 7.5 cm / 厘米
Artist's collection 藝術家收藏

Luminous Horizons 燦爛地平線
2020, Mixed media on canvas 布本混合媒介
101 x 151 x 7.5 cm / 厘米
Artist's collection 藝術家收藏

Flashes in Shadow 陰影裏的閃光
2020, Mixed media on canvas 布本混合媒介
101 x 151 x 7.5 cm / 厘米
Artist's collection 藝術家收藏

Floating Mountains 浮山
2019, Mixed media on canvas 布本混合媒介
61.6 x 91.5 x 7.5 cm / 厘米
Artist's collection 藝術家收藏

Expansive Evening Lights 擴大暮色
2019, Mixed media on canvas 布本混合媒介
61.6 x 91.5 x 7.5 cm / 厘米
Artist's collection 藝術家收藏

Twilight Mirror 曙光鏡子
2019, Mixed media on canvas 布本混合媒介
61.6 x 91.5 x 7.5 cm / 厘米
Artist's collection 藝術家收藏

Silver Mists 銀霧
2020, Mixed media on canvas 布本混合媒介
61.6 x 91.5 x 7.5 cm / 厘米
Artist's collection 藝術家收藏

Pigments Glimpsing Night 瞥見顏料之夜
2020, Mixed media on canvas 布本混合媒介
61.6 x 91.5 x 7.5 cm / 厘米
Artist's collection 藝術家收藏

Celestial Brushstrokes 天空筆觸
2020, Mixed media on canvas 布本混合媒介
61.6 x 91.5 x 7.5 cm / 厘米
Artist's collection 藝術家收藏

Crust of the Landscape 地形表殼
2020, Mixed media on canvas 布本混合媒介
35.6 x 65.5 x 7.5 cm / 厘米
Artist's collection 藝術家收藏

Chromatic Fantasies (Thinking of Jan Pieterszoon Sweelinck)
音階顏色狂想曲（想起揚・彼德松・思維林克）
2020, Mixed media on canvas 布本混合媒介
35.6 x 65.5 x 7.5 cm / 厘米
Artist's collection 藝術家收藏

Little Chromatic Fantasies I (Thinking of Jan Pieterszoon Sweelinck) 音階顏色小狂想曲之一（想起揚・彼德松・思維林克）
2020, Mixed media on canvas 布本混合媒介
11.8 x 21.8 x cm / 厘米
Artist's collection 藝術家收藏

Little Chromatic Fantasies II (Thinking of Jan Pieterszoon Sweelinck) 音階顏色小狂想曲之二（想起揚・彼德松・思維林克）
2020, Mixed media on canvas 布本混合媒介
7.1 x 13.1 cm / 厘米
Artist's collection 藝術家收藏

Merging Music and Landscape (Thinking of Unico Wilhelm van Wassenaer)
音樂與風景結合（想起尤奈高・威林・瓦瑟納爾）
2020, Mixed media on canvas 布本混合媒介
20.5 x 30.5 cm / 厘米
Artist's collection 藝術家收藏

Light Mist 光霧
2020, Mixed media on canvas 布本混合媒介
20.5 x 30.5 cm / 厘米
Artist's collection 藝術家收藏